Vincentia Schroeder, Margit Koemeda-Lutz (Eds.)
Bioenergetic Analysis 2010 (20)

»edition psychosozial«

Vincentia Schroeder, Margit Koemeda-Lutz (Eds.)

Bioenergetic Analysis

The Clinical Journal of the International Institute
for Bioenergetic Analysis (2010) Volume 20

Psychosozial-Verlag

Bibliographic information of Die Deutsche Bibliothek (The German Library)
Die Deutsche Bibliothek lists this publication in the Deutsche Nationalbibliografie
(German National Bibliography). Detailed bibliographical data can be accessed
via internet (http://dnb.ddb.de).

Original edition
© 2010 Psychosozial-Verlag
E-Mail: info@psychosozial-verlag.de
www.psychosozial-verlag.de
Cover: Alexander Lowen, © Heiner Steckel
Draft design cover: Hanspeter Ludwig, Giessen
www.imaginary-world.net
Printed in Germany
ISBN 978-3-8379-2044-4

Contents

Reviewers for this issue were:
Paula Buckley
Garry Cockburn
Maê Nascimento
Tarra Stariell

Letter from the Editor

Welcome to the twentieth volume of the clinical journal of the International Institute for Bioenergetic Analysis. Our founder, Alexander Lowen, died peacefully in his home at the age of 98. He died in October, 2008, shortly before we finalized the 2009 issue.

To honor Dr. Lowen, this volume contains memorial notes from some members of the IIBA community.

IIBA faculty and long-time member of the Board of Directors, David Finlay, also died in 2008. His article on intimate connections, introduced by Maê Nascimento, is included in this issue.

There are three original papers from our international members. On the topic of the wisdom of the failing body, is an article by Louise Fréchette, adapted from her keynote presentation at the Southern California Bioenergetic Conference in March of 2009. Louise is from Canada. Our other original works are also from authors outside the USA. Fina Pla, from Spain, considers issues related to gender and identity. Mariano Pedroza, from Brazil, writes on issues related to working bioenergetically within a community model in economically disadvantaged areas.

A new feature this year is translations of the abstracts of the three original articles. Some of our members do not read in English. In order to honor the international character of our community, we provide these translations in five languages besides English. These languages are German, Spanish,

Italian, Portuguese and French. I would like to thank the dedicated group of translators who worked on this project: Louise Fréchette and France Kauffman (French); Camile Milagres and Mariano Pedroza (Portuguese); Rosaria Filoni (Italian); Fina Pla and Edith Liberman (Spanish); and Margit Koemeda (German).

I would like to thank those who reviewed the articles this year: Paula Buckley, Garry Cockburn, Maê Nascimento, and Tarra Stariell. I thank Steve Schroeter for re-typing the original scanned version of David Finlay's paper. I send my loving gratitude to my core editorial support group of Maê Nascimento and Margit Koemeda.

You may feel sad reading memorial notes, intrigued with ideas from articles, and happy at moments of discovery. To be able to experience a myriad of varied feelings is part of feeling truly alive. This capacity to feel deeply, is the backbone of Alexander Lowen's life work. Through his theory and practice of Bioenergetics, he helped us learn how to define, promote, and value *feeling deeply*, and thereby, *living fully*. May this small volume contribute to moments of deeply felt aliveness for you.

Vincentia Schroeter
November 15, 2009

Memorial Notes about Alexander Lowen

The following are reflections on the personal and professional legacy of our founder, Dr. Alexander Lowen. Three are written for this volume, while the rest are excerpts from speeches given at Dr. Lowen's Memorial, April, 2009, in New York.

Alexander Lowen, May 2005, © Heiner Steckel

Tribute to Alexander Lowen

"Never let anybody make you doubt about what you feel!"

Guy Tonella

The first workshop I did with Dr. A. Lowen had such impact on me that I decided to initiate my bioenergetic training and travel to New York to start a therapy with him. That was in 1979, exactly 30 years ago, when I was in the bosom of psychoanalysis. This experience was a turning point in my life and my personal life.

What did Alexander Lowen have that was so special?

He was a therapist fully identified with its own conviction that the energy sequestered in bodily tensions depleted the ability to be alive, to love, to create. He drew from his acting conviction an impressive force, a presence of warrior that my resistances and defenses could never damage. He was demanding, he never compounded, he provoked me every time to express my fears, my anger, and my vitality to the limit of bearable. His penetrating blue eyes, sometimes challenging, sometimes tender, remained focused on my body expressiveness: the only reliable truth. He provoked me to perceive, feel, understand and change. I am deeply grateful.

One day, making me doubt during a session about what I was feeling, him perhaps having a different impression than mine, he saw my distress and said: "Guy, never let anybody make you doubt about what you feel when your feeling forces itself upon you!" He was just proposing to me that I trust in myself. I owe him since that day that constant search for deep identification with myself, with my own experience, my own perceptions and my own convictions.

I have rarely seen someone identified as much with himself and not with external events or people passing. I remember this Christmas, 1979, invited to stay at his home with his family: Leslie, his wife and Fred, his son. I remember that Al was the same there as in his office in New York. He was with this permanent concern of being oneself. He was not perfect but it was rooted in his being himself. This has been for me and forever an ethical model of life.

Lowen was a modern man, an observer of great intelligence and vision. I think he founded bioenergetic analysis around two central paradigms: 1) body-mind continuity builds from a basic, fundamental bodily identity, and 2) physical exercise combined with emotional expression provides sources of vitality, and continuously repairs and revitalizes somatic tissues and neuro-biological circuits. Neuroscience now scientifically legitimizes this approach. I work today, as many of us do, to build on the invaluable legacy he left us. My gratitude to him is immense, and my thoughts are constantly inspired by the experience that he made me live and the invaluable work he wrote.

Of course, my own history, my own personality, and my own culture commit me to developing and practicing bioenergetic analysis with my personal convictions and style, coherent with who I am. I also owe Alexander Lowen for what he said to me: "Make your own way, not trying to imitate me. If you stay grounded in your body, you will do your own discoveries."

Committing me today and for the future years in a mission backed by the United Nations Organization towards the peoples who suffer, I take my bioenergetic practice in my suit-case and I think to you, Al, to my heart you opened which can now receive the others and give, share and love. Thank you.

Al Lowen Memorial, May 2009

Helen Resneck-Sannes

The reason we are here today is that a great man, Al Lowen, died. He was charismatic, intelligent, passionate, a truly great thinker and writer, and attracted a group of intelligent and creative followers, some of whom you see here today. And the bottom line is that Al Lowen practiced and lived his ideas. He was as they say: "the real deal".

He accomplished something that had never been done before, and even though it looks simple, the brilliance of his theory is in its simplicity. By describing the functional unity of the body/mind, he provided operational definitions for such abstract concepts like grounding, energy, aliveness, depression, and gave them a physical description that matched their imagistic, metaphorical, and cognitive counterparts. In this sense he was a true behavioral psychologist. In The Language of the Body he described the muscular and energetic components (color, breath, contact, warmth) of different emotions and emotional defenses.

He also outlined the developmental relational environment in which these processes occurred, emphasizing the first three years of life. Many of his theories and descriptions of various attachment styles and consequences are now being validated by neuroscientific research. His analysis of the body's defense responses have been elaborated and developed in theories of trauma and therapeutic interventions for the treatment of trauma. Also, somatic schools of psychotherapy have been developed in the United States, i.e. Hakomi, Family Systems Therapy, without ever acknowledging that the theoretical basis for their systems is straight out of bioenergetics.

Al's passing generated many reactions, some of which you have heard today. I had a series of intense e-mail communication with Bob Lewis recently, and in the process of those interchanges, I began to remember the few times that I spent with Al. Let me tell you about such a time. I think like many of us, I like to feel in control of my reactions, which is why I especially like grounding because it calms me and I feel more in control. During one session with Al, he did everything he could to unground me, kicking my feet out from under me, and aggressively charging at me. It was at dinner after that session, in which I was having a difficult time managing the intense sexual charge and longing that had opened, he sat down next to me, looked me in the eyes and said: you can't control this through "will". My thought at the time, although I didn't say it to him, was that if I don't control this with my "will" I'll end up in jail for having too much fun, for being lewd and lascivious, arrogant and manipulative, and downright obnoxious. I couldn't imagine any other possibility than control.

Now, I think that we live in a synchronous universe, especially when something significant happens which affects your mind/body in it's core. Just after being invited to speak on this panel, a client e-mailed me this quote. He said that what Lowen wrote about the concept of "will" struck him deeply. Now, listen to these words. Lowen gives concrete references to abstract terms, such that we are impacted and know their deepest meaning.

Here is the quote:

> "Every painful situation is an emergency to which a person reacts via the sympathetic-adrenal system by increasing his state of tension and of hyper-tonicity in the muscles as they prepare to act ... the heightened consciousness involves an active engagement of the 'will'. In an emergency an individual doesn't act spontaneously; every action is a calculated move designed to remove the danger" (p. 57).

This quote came out of the book, Pleasure, and not until my client brought me this quote, did I really understand what Al was trying to tell me that evening. We can't truly be open to the streaming of energy, and I have had the experience of surrendering to that wonderful sensation, albeit for brief times (but then again, they are always way too brief). But my real point is that "will" is not an abstract fuzzy concept. He explains how "will" appears in the body as hypertonicity in the muscles, a heightened consciousness, and I would include, self consciousness.

Al showed the way by writing in such clear, embodied, operational, knowable terms how to find our selves. Hopefully, his work will not vanish into "The Mists of Avalon", a heroic legend talked about as just that a myth, but it's true impact, long forgotten. That is my fear, so I continue to expand my knowledge and practice of Bioenergetics, bringing in the relational aspects and the new information from trauma theories, but never forgetting Al's gift, to reach and extend, to ground what we know and do in the physical world, that can be experienced and known in the concrete reality of our body/selves.

I thank you all.

Excerpts from speeches given in April, 2009, at the Memorial for Alexander Lowen, in New York

Bob Lewis

Al set an example for us all in how he both remained deeply true to his Reichian roots and still found his own way. He was both deeply loyal to Reich and yet did not canonize/mummify his teachings, but rather infused them with his own inspiration, and his own creative center: Al systematized character analysis, extending Reich's theories to all the different character types. He further delineated the character dynamics psychologically and physically and described their libidinal connections. Al developed expressive exercises, and got his patients onto their feet, developing the basic Bioenergetic concept of grounding.

I am suggesting that, as an institute, we can best honor Al Lowen by following his example. That is, to engage in the ongoing challenge of remaining true to our Bioenergetic roots, without rigidifying the truths they hold such that we are no longer a living body of artisans. As Al modeled for us, we can reach for a Bioenergetic institute that moves from and is inspired both by what Al inherited from Reich, what he added to the Bioenergetic work in progress and what we each in turn bring to it.

In this room today, and in our institute at large, I thank God that we do not all see things the same way. There may be those who feel that they practice a version of bioenergetics that is truer and more loyal, to Al's fundamental vision. Others, like myself, still believe we are true members of the guild, even though we incorporate into our clinical work ways of understanding and being with patients which were not Al's ways. What I do hope that we all share, and what Scott Baum described as foundational in his recent inaugural presidential message to us, is a commitment to keeping our patients' (and our own) somatopsychic unity or lack of it, at the heart of our clinical encounters. This was Reich's enduring gift to us: the functional identity of a person's character and his bodily attitude. It will not go out of style.

Looking back, I want to bear witness to the tremendous vitality and hope that Al inspired in those of us in his presence. His sparking blue eyes, a resonant timber in his voice, and the sureness of his touch and his words ... his was the stuff of psychosomatic charisma – his inner fire burned bright. Add to this the loving synergy that moved between Al and John Pierrakos at the informal Tuesday night clinical seminars, and it was indeed a special time in the young life of bioenergetics.

There has also been something about Al's tolerance of our contributions that has made possible the vitality of our Institute. Forgive me for mentioning only three among many examples of this vitality – First, our revised, state of the art 2005 Bioenergetic training curriculum put together by Violaine de Clerck, Guy Tonella and Odila Weigand – Second, the clinical treasures in the Bioenergetic Reader (2008) put together under Vita Heinrich's leadership and Third, the exciting work that continues to come out in our Journal, edited by Vincentia Schroeter, Margit Koemeda-Lutz and Maê Nascimento. We are indeed a worldwide Bioenergetic community that lives, breathes and pulsates.

I believe Al's teaching, his wisdom and legacy to us were about what he did for most of his life. His central passion was about healing the mind-body split, and his chosen path to this goal was his own self-exploration. In the process, he gave us the gift of a passionate exploration of and brilliant illumination of the endless facets of the mind-body's unity and duality of function. He did this, arguably as not even Reich had done, and, less arguably, as no one after him will likely do.

It is possible, but not likely, that someone will emerge from among us post-Lowenian bioenergeticists who will be able to lead us with the force of certainty about his truth that emanated from Freud, Reich and Lowen himself. It is not likely that anyone will soon match Al's passion for and genius at knowing a person in and from the pulse of their body. It will be interesting to see what kind of therapeutic outcomes and unforeseen partnerships may arise as our patients sense that, even though we do the best we can to read in their psyche-soma the person that they are, we cannot see into their deepest recesses with the same conviction in the clarity of our vision. Sensing that we need help to unveil (unravel) the mystery that they are, they may have to engage with us in a slow, implicit, mutual process of discovery.

Vivian Guze

Al Lowen's life spanned most of the 20th century, and he died just short of his 98th birthday toward the end of 2008. His life passion was sparked when he heard Wilhelm Reich lecture at the New School for Social Research in 1940. These lectures shook him to his bones and set the tone for his entire career. He was about 30 years old. He started his practice of therapy in New York in 1951. The decade of the 1950's was a very repressive time in this country. The fear of being non conformist or being called a communist by Senator McCarthy hung like a dark cloud over the intellectual community of the U.S. Yet, at the same time, in isolated pockets, individual psychotherapists were incubating new ideas and ways of doing therapy that erupted in the next decade.

Al Lowen was a man of his time. His seminal work *"The Physical Dynamic of Character Structure"* was published in 1958.

I had worked in a mental hospital during the 1950's, when psychotherapy with psychotics was considered impossible. I began doing things like – squeezing a person's hand as I spoke, so I could hold her attention a few seconds longer. But I had no colleagues to talk with about it. Then I got a flyer announcing open professional Bioenergetic demonstrations in Dr. Alexander Lowen's office. I went. And, here I am.

As I said, Al Lowen was a man of his time. His work jarred with mainstream inhibitions about sex and strong emotional expression. During the 60's, Al went out to speak to many groups – always embattled by hecklers and negative mainstream discussants. Then he'd go out and do it, and again and again meet a wall of negativity. Those of us who watched, felt that it took heroic dedication and energy in the service of the Right as he experienced his Mission. He was a hero, a genuine hero, a warrior. A warrior fights fiercely for what he believes, and, at his best, fights for the help, protection and healing of those he cares about. All said he was not a revolutionary, the way Reich was, but in his own way he was. He was not afraid to be different, and unlike Reich, his focus was not to change society but to stay within the arena of character analysis and physical work to recover the aliveness and dignity of the individual. This was his mission. I took courage from his battles, and my battles were easier, because of him. For this I am deeply, deeply grateful.

In later years, when Al Lowen felt that some of his followers were not doing Bioenergetic Analysis the way he wanted them to, he forgot something he had told me early on. I had complained that I couldn't do something in therapy the way he did. His reply was: "Bioenergetics moves through each person's body in a unique way. So of course, your way of doing therapy won't be like mine." I have held on to this statement through the years, no matter what he said later. I have felt secure in the knowledge that whatever moves through my body is bioenergetics.

In 1971, at the end of a workshop, I was sitting next to Al when he said, "come with me". I followed him into the next room, where there were a group of people assembled, and there I learned that we were going to teach in a formal program. Since I had never been his patient, I couldn't tell how he felt about me, and was surprised when he invited me in. As more and more people became involved in Bioenergetics, through the training programs, Al became uneasy, since he mainly trusted only what he could touch. And like Reich he had little faith in organizations of any kind. 1972–73 was a very difficult year for Al and those of us in the inner group who met monthly in his office. That was the year John Pierrakos, his long term office partner, started to push for adding a spiritual dimension to the Bioenergetic work. Al was opposed to moving in any direction away from the physical body. Within a year, John left the Bioenergetic Institute and formed what he called, Core Energetics. Al was deeply hurt and angry at the defection. As a warrior he was so convinced of the rightness of his own position that he became infuriated whenever he was challenged. And here it was his own partner who challenged him. It took over 20 years before he allowed a rapprochement to take place.

Over time, Bioenergetics spread from the U.S. to Europe and then to South America. By the middle 90's, the warrior had started to feel ungrounded in his life. It was time to withdraw from the fray, to rest and recover his strength, so he resigned as Director of the IIBA, at age 86, but continued his practice and to give workshops.

In the course of things, I was disappointed that he disregarded women's issues. But I was used to that. I come from a generation of women who, if we wanted something, went to where it was, absorbed what we could and threw away the rest. One time, Al was holding forth our group of seven psychiatrists and me. He looked as if he was in a movie version of a 19 century surgical arena, the big professor dispensing knowledge and wisdom to the doctors and medical students. As he strode up and down, he intoned, "Gentlemen", and continued with his talk. John Bellis quickly glanced at me. I, of course, didn't move a muscle. I shall always cherish the memory of John Bellis for that involuntary movement. On the other hand, Al was always respectful of me on a personal level, as he was respectful of all his women patients with whom I have spoken.

What I have appreciated most about Al Lowen was the clarity of his thinking, the carefulness of his boundaries, his courage in pursuing his mission, his gracefulness on the dance floor, and his unwillingness to engage in disputes and controversy about other systems of therapy. I admired the physicalness in his spirituality. While he responded with awe at the vastness of nature and the mystery of the life force, he also insisted that Grace consisted of resilience and harmony in the form and movement of the body. He never achieved the softness he aspired to, as part of his concept of Grace, and he never achieved the grand influence in the medical community that he originally fancied. Yet, he succeeded in living his life according to his principles. His teachings gave legitimacy to the field of body psychotherapy, he gave people like me a place to be, where I could feel at home as a therapist who used her hands and her breath as tools. To almost the end of his life, Al kept his own tools honed, thinking up new ways of working energetically, like the Samurai of old, whose first duty was to keep their swords sharpened.

In conclusion, Al Lowen fulfilled his nature. He lived his life with honour and integrity, and left us with some clues about how we might live ours, hopefully, with a deeper, though imperfect understanding along whatever paths we take from the road he carved out.

Heiner Steckel

To be able to feel your feelings, to express them and to be able to contain – was the triad Al Lowen claimed for a solid body based identity. And that is, what his work was about …

Over a period of 30 years I saw Al Lowen in individual sessions and workshops – and later travelling with him, when he had asked me to help him at international Conferences. And I remember waking up in the morning by these dull rhythmic beats, when Al was kicking in the hotel-room next door. … Al practiced what he was suggesting to others … helping me and others experience and understand our selves deeper.

A therapeutic moment: Here I was on the stool – and my chest wasn't moving too much. He: "You need to cry" … me: "I know" and he: "So why don't you cry then; to whom you don't want to show your tears?" and here was the experienced patient: "To my mother" … Al: "I don't see your mother in this room – and I am asking myself how long you want to bring her here, in order not to be alive." So, he did relate and he understood transference … he deeply understood how relational experiences of our childhood left the marks in our physiology, shaped our body and can rule and ruin our relationships here and now. These incorporations are the base for negative self-concepts and became the base for repetition patterns and transferencial hang-ups. As Al liked to say, the protective castle of the child turns into the prison of the adult. I always found this such a simple and true metaphor for the concept of character structure. … I am so grateful having experienced Al Lowen many times – relating to me and others from his deep faith in the biological resources of the human animal, from his deep understanding of the vulnerable wounded human animal, from his deep conviction in life and passion for life, and from his trust in the energetic processes, with which we can restore our bodily-self and heal. You must find and re-connect to your animal nature to be fully human. This was his credo I heard many times. And for him this was at the core of humanity. And for me this is at the core of my Bioenergetics understanding and practice.

I was also with him in very difficult moments, when he suffered from the disrespect he felt from his own school, when he witnessed a movement away from what he considered the center and base of Bioenergetic work. He himself had the courage to question the characterology he had developed as in danger of being misused to categorize people instead of being seen as a tool for deeper understanding of the individual's dynamic ... At the same time many colleagues in the Institute felt the need to integrate more of a psychodynamic point of view. This was not an easy moat to bridge. Probably because of personal issues involved on both sides, it seemed incompatible. It certainly became a wound to him – not easy to heal. I witnessed that Al could see and own his part in it. He expressed this in several personal conversations we had. In certain moments he even regretted that he had founded a school and organization. I disagreed, because I wouldn't be here today, if there hadn't been a school. And I wish for us, engaged in this school, that in our maturation and differentiation, we can stay deeply connected to the roots and honouring them, no matter on which branches of the Bioenergetics tree we may be.

Let us have a look at a very material part of the legacy. I look to Al's writings, from where we can make a seamless connection to the findings of modern neurobiology, emotion and trauma research. He still reaches people in the way he wrote, touches human bodies and becomes personally very meaningful for many of them. I personally look into the books again and again, finding them stimulating, enriching and convincing. This heritage is a treasure, a gold mine, which has not yet been fully exploited (explored).

Al Lowen trusted that we can take care of ourselves, when we reconnect and refer to our organismic being and by this to our self-healing forces and capacities. This is also in the core of my Bioenergetics understanding and practice.

Al loved Greece, Greek wine, Metaxa, its music and dance. And the last very special dance we had was when I was sitting next to him, – the last time I saw him – and Monica and Fred put on Greek music and his vitality and joy was there with the rhythm and the movements, which were still possible.

Dear Al, I miss you with all I have mentioned and more ... Thank you.

Alice Ladas

While I say a few words about my 55 year connection with Dr Alexander Lowen and his work, I would like you to stand. The purpose is to honor one of Al's major contributions to the field of psychotherapy: getting clients to stand on their feet. Al was the very first therapist in the west to use the words "bio-energy" to describe his work. 60 plus years later, energy psychology and energy medicine are just beginning to emerge.

In 1955, Al was speaking at a facility and I was introducing him and suggested to Al and John Pierrakos that becoming a non-profit institute might be useful. In 1956, at their request, I hired lawyer Robert Sturz, to help us form the Institute for Bioenergetic Analysis. In 1957 I introduced Al to publisher Henry Stratton. The result was the publication in 1958 of *"The Physical Dynamics of Character Structure"*, Al's first book.

Working with Al set the course for the remainder of my professional and personal life, and for this I am profoundly grateful. It may sound self serving to mention the projects that grew out of my work with Al, but what students do because of their mentors is, in my opinion, the greatest tribute to the mentor. So I am going to take that risk.

Graduating from the second training group, I began work as a Bioenergetic therapist and continue that today. But I was also inspired to help women reclaim the right to use their bodies as they wish to. Reich and Al convinced me of the importance of the birth experience for infant and mother, so I studied and then taught the first Lamaze course in the USA.

My doctoral dissertation, "*Breastfeeding, the Less Available Option*", was inspired, in part, by Al's emphasis on the importance of breastfeeding. With the help of 1100 members of the *La Leche League* and publication in 4 peer reviewed journals, the study helped to turn the tide back towards breastfeeding in the USA. And of course I breastfed our daughters for the three years Al prescribed! We quit by verbal agreement.

In 1982, I helped create a synthesis of the work of the Freudians and the sex researchers in the book, "*The G Spot and Other Discoveries About Human Sexuality*". Appendix B contains a synopsis of "*Women and Bioenergetic Analysis*". This research, done with my late husband, Harold Ladas, was inspired by women Bioenergetic analysts who, in 1977, began meeting separately from the men. As a result, some information about Bioenergetic Analysis has reached over a million people in 19 languages and 28 countries. Getting the Bioenergetic research included in "*The G Spot*" book was a personal struggle.

Today I lead the research committee on the board of the U.S. Association for Body Psychotherapy because one of the initial stated purposes of the IIBA was research. Cheerleading for research is also a tribute to another Bioenergetic mentor, the late Dr John Bellis, the first Bioenergetic trainer to suggest including a research project in the training of CBTs. The research prizes awarded by the USABP have been won by several Bioenergetic therapists, including Christa Ventling, Margit Koemeda-Lutz, Martin Kaschke, Dirk Revenstorf, Thomas Scherrmann, Halko Weiss and Ulrich Soeder.

If Al was, at times, somewhat patriarchal and less focused on the relational, he should be given lots of slack. His acceptance of the work of other therapists, his listening to his patients, was far in advance of anything done by his mentor, Reich. If Al was not enthusiastic about research, it was because our culture was already too focused on the intellect while surpressing feelings.

I believe Al was a genius at reading our way of being from our bodies. It is another of the major things he taught us and while he was a good teacher, he was the genius and we mere students.

George Downing

Summarized here are four suggestions for the future proposed in my Memorial weekend talk.

1. Continued systematic development of new ideas. To take just one example, the new thinking about the therapeutic relationship, developed by trainers other than Al (Bob Hilton, Bob Lewis, and others), seems to me today one of the Institute's important strengths. Even this strand alone needs further reflection. In all current psychotherapy, relational psychoanalysis included, we are probably just at the beginning of understanding what really takes place in the therapeutic exchange.

2. Preservation of the core teachings. Al had his own way to work and his own way to conceptualize it. Different in different periods, yet with substantial underlying continuity. This legacy remains precious, in my opinion.

Naturally any practitioner is going to pick and choose. She will adopt some elements of this repertoire and forego others. But the repertoire itself needs to be recognized as such and conscientiously transmitted. Arguments about "hard bioenergetics" and "soft bioenergetics" and all the rest will never stop, nor should they. At the same time the innovations put into place by Al himself merit to be passed on with respect and care.

3. Better communication of the "complex model". Al was a forceful and extremely successful spokesperson for bioenergetics for years upon years and the task was not easy.

How do you convey to persons who have never worked with the body, and never seen such work, what it is like and what it can bring? Al's solution, and probably the right one given the circumstances, was to simplify and condense. He delivered a stripped-down "simplified model". Whereas what we, in the Institute, know and appreciate might be called a "complex model", much more sophisticated with regard to both theory and practice.

The result, as I described at length in my talk, is that we now face a paradox. In one sense bioenergetics is widely known. And many of its components have been taken on board by other schools. On the other hand, those who have borrowed some elements tend to have an image of the Bioenergetic approach limited to the simplified model. Often they have little grasp of the more sophisticated framework, little sense that it even exists. The coming years might therefore be the right time to better convey the complex model to interested outsiders.

4. Archeology of the textual heritage, of Al's texts, I mean. Al wrote in different modes. Frequently he expressed himself in pithy, somewhat repetitive (to the Bioenergetic reader) statements. But at other times he let his thinking be more searching. It was more messy, in a good sense.

Some of these "implicit" probings, as Bob Lewis called them in his Memorial talk, or anyway half implicit, arguably deserve renewed attention. They merit discussion, explication, dismantling, reassemblage. Heiner Steckel in his Memorial contribution has made a similar comment. Again to take one example, The Language of the Body contains highly interesting perspectives on early parent-infant and parent-child interaction. And this was back in the fifties! It was at a time when almost no one else in psychotherapy was attempting to describe early transactions on so concrete a level! This was admirable, and much more could be said about it in the light of current developmental research. Other examples abound.

Bob Hilton

In 1968, when he delivered the William Alanson White Institute lectures (these lectures appear in the wonderful little book, Psychoanalytic Theory, Therapy and the Self), Harry Guntrip said in his introduction, "There is something wrong with us if our theoretical ideals remain stagnant and impervious to change for too long. Theory is simply the best we can do to date to conceptualize the experiences of our patients present with us." He also states, "To care for people is more important than to care for ideas, which can be good servants but bad masters."

Freud broke away from his contemporaries. Reich did this with Freud and Lowen with Reich. Part of the creative genius of an innovator is the passion he has about his work, which is fueled by his own personality needs.

The followers of any great leader always face the problem of ferreting out the universal principles for which the leader stands over, against the leader's own personal idiosyncrasies. When individual personality needs and cultural influences are not considered and an attempt is made to hold on to what is conceived as an "original truth", then orthodoxy and fundamentalism develop, where doctrine and theory become more important than people.

So what does this say about the future of Bioenergetics? I see our task as supporting the legacy of the principles for which Lowen stood which apply to us all, and our future is in having room for discussion and presentation of those aspects of Bioenergetics that we have needed to change in order to address our personal needs and those of our clients. Lowen said he was drawn to Reich because he represented a therapy with a body/mind connection. He also said that Reich's tragedy was that he wasn't oriented toward grounding. As we are all aware, grounding became a major emphasis in Bioenergetic therapy. Just as Lowen added grounding to his Reichian therapy we as Bioenergetic therapists today are faced with how to integrate our current understanding of the healing process of the mind/body split with the basic Bioenergetic principles we have been taught. Our future lies in the success of that process of integration.

But I must ask the question, "What might keep us from embodying, and realizing that future?" Part of the answer to that question comes from the nature of our contributions. Since our insights come out of our need for intimacy and attachment, which were not provided for in our original theories, we now have a narcissistic investment in maintaining our system of interpretation. Our theories, as well as those of Freud, Reich and Lowen, can function as a narcissistic defense against the feelings of shame, humiliation and impotence. To have our theories challenged or to have them fall on deaf ears may be to open up the wounds from which these theories sprang.

I have had, as have you, many powerful energetic experiences with Al. But one of the most profound experiences came from a simple comment he made one day while working with me. I was sitting on the floor in his office having just exhausted myself with expressions of terror and grief from my early childhood, when he said, "Bob, this never should have happened to you." We know today through the study of neurobiology why hearing these words was such a powerful Bioenergetic experience. But apart from the explanation of how his limbic brain was talking to my limbic brain, I then knew that I was a person, not my character or my problem, but I, as Bob, impacted him in such a way that he would share the pain and love of his heart with me at that moment. It has been my experience that when such a confirming love is given and received, a spontaneous movement begins in our bodies that leads us back toward recovering our lost identity and vitality. For me, the Bioenergetic grounding exercises did not hold up until I found grounding in the gracious and heartfelt relationships I have had with my therapists over the years. For me, this makes Bioenergetic therapy less about going from the outside in and more about coming from the inside out.

The future of Bioenergetics is already here in this room. The embodiment of that future is in our hands or, I should rather say, in our hearts. It lies in our capacity to put aside our commitment to a theory and embrace the life from which the theory sprang. In his autobiography, Al says, "Bioenergetics aims to help a person open his heart and love. But if the objective is not gained, the result is tragic." I want to thank Al for his acknowledging that in the gracious sharing of an open heart is the future of Bioenergetics.

Memorial Note

Eleanor Greenlee

Alexander Lowen was an incredible man! His contribution to the concept of how the body affects the mind and the mind affects the body was revolutionary and expanded psychotherapy into psycho-somatic psychotherapy. In my opinion, he brought into psychology the awareness of the body, the body's correlations to our mental problems and how to work with the physical aspects of our emotional problems.

I first met Al when he came to California in the early 1970's to my training program. He was powerful in his presence and in his work. He showed us how the body revealed its areas of chronic muscular tension and how to work with it. Right then and there I said, "We are going to invite this man to come and train for us every time he can" and he did come often. We found out that he liked skiing in the winter and warm climates in the summer. We arranged every possible training that would appeal to him so we could benefit from his genius. Most of all he helped us start a walk on our path to health and well-being.

For me working with Al was not easy, but created transformation into an existence of truly living my body without most of the restrictions of my past traumatic experiences.

Anyone who worked with him knows he demanded you give your all, but painful as it was, the journey was worth the trip. Initially, he scared the heck out of me but not in the same way that negative experiences of my past life had affected me. It was a feeling of being "scared to move into the unknown", but the outcome was worth the journey.

Al demanded a lot and he gave a lot! I remember the last time I worked with him, this time both of us sharing the responsibility of working with people. I thank the powers that be that made it possible and for the gift of Al's acceptance of me. God Bless Him, and I hope the angels up in heaven are ready for him.

I love him dearly.

A Key Therapeutic Experience
with Alexander Lowen

Phil M. Helfaer

I experienced Al as a healing presence during the period I saw him for therapy. In one particular session, I made the unexpected discovery of the experience of self-respect. I no longer remember the content of the session. I remember suddenly becoming quiet, just standing in the room with Al, who was sitting in the chair beside me. Probably I had been on the stool, maybe crying. I was aware of Al's supportive and unobtrusive presence. Then I got it. I was me, just myself. All the terrible self-judgments and shameful self-attributions fell away, and for a moment disappeared. Here I was, "just" in my body, with all my sorrows, faults, and pain, but I had myself with – and, in my mind, there is only one word for it– self-respect.

I was never inclined to use the term "self-esteem", which has a psychological cast to it, as if I were, in my mind, esteeming my-self mentally as another object. What I experienced felt like a simpler state and a deeper one, a bodily way of being. In that state of being I could tolerate the terrible affects that had assailed me, the shame, the humiliation, and the deep agonies of loss and abandonment. A year or so later (1984), I "found my-self" giving a paper on "Sex and Self-Respect" at one of the conferences, and, never suspecting the concept of self-respect would become a life-long companion, published a book some years later using the term in the title (Helfaer 1998, 2006, Bioenergetics Press).

How was I able to reach this healing experience in my work with Al at this particular moment? I found it in myself, of course; it emerged from my work. I believe, however, the experience was enabled by Al's presence. If he were not somehow in a state to enable or be with it, I doubt that it would have happened. For one thing, he didn't get too busy with me too quickly to allow for the time for the feeling experience to emerge and form. I felt from him an empathy for my suffering, I felt seen by him, and I experienced him as a positive presence, a companion in my aloneness.

I believe there was also another more specific element in his way of being with me which I would identify as a kind of *respect for me as a living body*. I feel that this kind of respect and feel for the living body is quite rare. For him, "I am my body", had a real meaning. That meaning and that respect had registered within me, and at that moment I had my own experience of those states of being, and that experience fostered my healing path.

Memorial Note about David J. Finlay

Maê Nascimento

It was 1996, when I first met David at the IIBA international conference in Pocono, United States. I was – still reluctantly, coming back from a time away from Bioenergetics. He was visiting "home" (United States) coming from far New Zealand, where he was living and working as the coordinator trainer for a Bioenergetic training program. That was the beginning of a connection which would grow bigger and closer.

He was a brilliant man, passionate and profound in everything he put himself into, and Bioenergetics and the IIBA had not been exceptions. As a man of ideas and ideals, he wanted to bring fresh air into the field and his passion to the community. On his thoughts upon theoretical terms of Bioenergetics, he had always been in favor of expansion and integration of new ideas and, for that, things were not often smooth for him. His work within the institution aimed to deepen consciousness and to make things happen based in high principles and ideals. I was able to witness much of his struggle to keep things together, but this task had never been easy and for that he paid a high price, even affecting his health.

Well, he also had his temper and was not always easy to get along with, but his sense of loyalty and fairness were way beyond his flaws.

He was someone to be trusted, no matter what, and contributed with his mind and soul in trying to make of our world a better place to live. For that he garnered great respect and admiration from everybody who got to know him.

He was a man of the world and whenever he would stay somewhere a bit longer he would feel restless – there would always be another place to get to know and to be explored. For this reason – and for his lack of ability with languages (alleged by himself often) he did not stay living in Brazil. But this had never prevented our sense of togetherness in some way. With us, intimacy was always there and, no matter how long we might stay without being together in person, each time we met it was like we had never been apart. We knew what thoughts we had in mind just by looking into each other's eyes and this is not a small thing.

I have never doubted that it had been by his inspiration that I came back to Bioenergetics, where I have known some of my dearest friends from abroad.

David left this world in April of 2008, but for those who had the privilege of his friendship, his presence had been so strong, that he will live forever in their minds and hearts as an inspiration. He will certainly live in mine, in a very special way as an everlasting intimate connection.

Notes on Intimate Connections

David J. Finlay

Intimacy is an **Art of Creation** – a celebration of aliveness. It is a state where we can feel understood, safe, physically strong and capable, able to empathize and help others. Through intimacy our fears can be tamed. Intimacy as a way of harmony may be our best chance of finding our way home on levels ranging from the cellular to the soul, personally and interpersonally, perhaps even nationally and internationally.

Many of us have histories of broken connections, often beginning in infancy when "Mom and Dad" were not there the way we needed. Our lives became a search for finding close connections within ourselves, to others, to life as a whole. Often we did so without guiding principles around connection and attunement to the various environments in which we lived and functioned. Our search occasionally led to increased desperateness, with despair or death lurking in the background. However, as Au and Canon point out, "When intimacy is accompanied by love, it can become a crucible for our wholeness, stirring up what needs to be integrated and holding us in love as we meet those parts of ourselves which we have feared and hated", Depending on our personal "condition", then, we can offer only what we have. But we can create much more if we open our hearts and souls.

What is intimacy? Simply put it is IN-TO-ME-SEE. Paul Tillich described such a condition: "We can discover our souls only through the mirror of those who look at us." If so, the plea is: Give me the gift of your empathetic eyes so that I, too, can see. If you see me, then by the same privilege perhaps I can see you and myself as well. We can meet for we both have this basic and passionate human need. And if we meet perhaps we can engage. If we engage, perhaps we can connect from deeper places within ourselves.

In that connection we will have created something different than each of us. In that synthesis or synergy lies a new and expanded life form. If we nurture it, care and tend and give to it, there will be an engagement with life forces. They will encourage similar processes elsewhere perhaps even expanding geometrically and with possibilities of quantum leaps into a sense of partnership, communion and community. But dare I let *you* see into me? Dare we create something between us that heals our broken connections and allows our souls to vibrate and *resonate, to* touch and engage? That would be intimacy.

The miracle of this process of intimacy is no secret, no hidden truth that only some privileged or enlightened few attain. We can see it plainly most days if we observe, if we are receptive to looking and seeing. For example, it is in the healthy bond between mother and infant, the absolute miracle of conception, birth and growth. It is in the germinating seed of life-the little "wiggler" that scores a bull's eye and begins the process of conception, a growth process that can last forever until death and perhaps beyond. In that **energetic embrace of life** lies the truth of intimate connection.

In this small essay I ruminate on various aspects of intimacy certainly not in a definitive way. I explore, however familiar to others, but as a new expression for me. I shall consider thoughts about how body and self are connected; how intimacy is related to idealized images; how love and hate are joined in a desperate path; the loaded relationship between intimacy and sexuality and the ensuing confusion; the therapeutic relationship and the limitations of the pathology model; and finally, the nature of intimacy in terms of ego-psychology.

I   The Bodyself

Part of the capacity for intimacy is based on our bodyself-the images and distortions, truth and lies, conscious or unconscious, we believe about ourselves. In coming into the world our Self was largely a body phenomenon. Our emergent or primary Self was connected to mother and our movements in relationship to her. We grasped with our hands, sucked with our lips and mouth, pushed with our feet, sought to focus our eyes, all toward re-establishing contact, a new contact outside the womb. We sought to communicate through our struggling movements, to tell the significant other of our needs. Those needs grew daily and our life-breath carried us forth on a journey of Self and Other discovery. To the extent that our physical and emotional needs were met we flourished, becoming ever more demanding of our environment to satisfy our new "I" and "We".

Being empathically responded to was our definition of intimacy and little by little in our primary narcissism we could give back in terms of recognition, delight and comfort. "You are my mother", we seemed to say, "and I have these needs you must fulfill and I'll try my best to let you know what they are. I shall meet your love, take it in and let you see YourSelf grow as a result. My system is totally open to you, but it must be treated with care. As you respond, so also will I. Isn't it wonderful that we can have this relationship where you can give fully of yourself and I can receive it to the limits of my capacities? And you'll be delighted with each movement I make in my development. We shall, of course, test each other so that our bonding will deepen and our attachment will unfold in the merry-go-round we are on. This beginning is only a moment in the memories that will fill our lives. This could be wonderful; as we separate, as I individuate, the nature of our relationship will change, but it will have been built on the solid foundation of an intimate connection."

We are a product of our socialization, the way we were raised and taught to view ourselves. We are also a product of our imagination as well as the imagination of others. Thus we now need to ask ourselves:

(1) How do I view my body as Self,
(2) How much of my emotional energy is directed toward liking/disliking my body as Self,
(3) What feelings and attitudes are built into the way I bodily present myself to the world? In what postures do I see myself? What happens to these postures as I physically move? Does it change my sense of Self and if so, how?
(4) If I dislike my body what does that protect me from or how does it help me?
(5) How has my body failed me? How have I failed my bodyself?
(6) And what steps, if any, am I willing to take to bring my "body" and "ego" selves together into unity rather than separation? Or do I plan to keep separate compartments for body and mind?

Although we may delude ourselves by separating mind and body, they work as a unit most of the time, at least at an emotional level. The intricacies of that interaction are only partially known in the worlds of biology, psychology, medicine and philosophy. It is still an open frontier of science. And if we had total knowledge of that interaction, what would we do with it? Would it change our behavior and values? In any case, our knowledge has not produced an intimate concern with the quality of life. Our primitiveness remains intact.

The bodyself we hold in our hearts and minds will be reflected in our social interactions at all levels of our being. When we look at our ego images and our body images, disparity is often a measure of disturbance. Weakness of the body image may be compensated for by exaggeration of the ego image (and vice versa). Alexander Lowen states there is a functional identity between the body image and the actual body. If we feel alive, robust and healthy, more than likely my body will be just that unless I live in a world of delusion. If, on the other hand, I conceive of myself as "ugly", I will probably withdraw my energy into my core and my aliveness will be absent. My heart will be less available to others. What is necessary in health is an inner and outer harmony and without this we are not fully available for intimate connections. But we must begin that process with openness of the Self, for herein lies the source and foundation of connectedness.

II   Idealized Intimacy

Idealization often takes place in the notion of "romantic love". With the blush of affection and budding sexuality everything seems perfect for we see through the passion of romance – exciting and wonderful, adventuresome and fanciful, sensuous and sexual. We see through the prisms of illusion and no matter what the age, there is an adolescent quality to it, but it is only a very first stage in the developing of intimacy. Sooner or later-about six months to a year – realities begin to emerge and then the catastrophe hits, the illusion or delusion has to be strengthened, or else persons begin the working through process where they must go deeper. It is then that questions of commitment arise, when tolerance and acceptance are truly joined. The achievement of intimacy is one thing, maintaining it another. Unfortunately, an adolescent attitude often gets prolonged. Romance can be sustained but only in a mature relationship. It requires hard work on both persons' part. But first it requires us to grow up from fantasy to the development of trust, friendship and support.

Scott Peck argues that in a mature relationship both partners have as an ultimate concern the psychological, physical, emotional and spiritual growth of the other. According to him this absolutely requires **attentive listening** – a total concentration on what the other is saying or trying to say in their expression. So often we hear or see only what we want particularly in conflict situations where listening is cut-off. We begin to formulate replies not on what is being said but on what may have previously happened. We filter information through the lens of what we believe to be true or not true. Our projections then lead to familiar responses and have little to do with attentive listening. We become prisoners of our own making.

To heal such rifts, according to Stephen and Ondrea Levine, requires the development of a "present heart", a heart that can let go of what we think we cannot accept, a letting go of obsessive "not enoughness" and the "frightened self". Instead we must allow the other's mind into our own hearts. To be fulfilling, such action requires reciprocation and mutuality. This is where sustained empathy comes in.

Empathy, simply defined, is the ability to see and feel the other-not to become them, but to resonate with them in an attuned way and to know their subjective experience without judgment. As we resonate, we also need to be open to disclosure, to accept the permeability and inter-penetrability of our being. Ego investment is the largest obstacle in this regard for that "I" has only one side and that is "me-ness".

The conscious or unconscious investment in "me-ness" leaves little room for an-other, however "beloved" we think our attitude is, however "altruistic" or deluded our self image may be. This is often true of person-alities who experienced early deprivations. They seldom get beyond their "me-ness", despite years of analysis or therapy and their consciousness is limited and their actions are sometimes bizarre. Woody Allen marrying his stepdaughter may be an illustration of extreme self-justification.

In the Big Book of Alcoholics Anonymous there is a passage, which states the following: **Serenity is inversely proportionate to expectations and directly proportionate to acceptance.** Expectations usually lead to disappointment, for so often they are based on hope such as the wish to be rescued or taken care of, to be cherished as though one were a child, or to have our neurotic strivings answered or fulfilled, etc. It is hope rather than faith because the former is illusory and the latter has some basis in reality. To be recognized as we wish and to be recognized as we are, too often has a great disjunction as therapists so often see in the consulting room.

Acceptance, on the other hand, can lead to a peace of mind for we are no longer, "director of the show". It connotes a consenting mind. Things are what they are and perhaps what they are meant to be. That does not mean that we accept everything for some things are just down-right unacceptable to our consciences or violate our distinguishing of right and wrong. But on a more mundane level we see people fighting in traffic to get one car length ahead of another, regardless of the danger they may create. There will always be insults and violations and acceptance may mean not participating or getting one's ego involved in the games of fools. We need to step back and relax, not submitting to the temptation to engage in such games as an equally neurotic participant. Acceptance is also the ability to receive, as well as work for, positive change.

There has to be in acceptance an attitude of forgiveness. When we operate or live without consciousness of this process, the temptation is to join the games whatever they may be- the pursuit of money, power, status, image, "winning", or whatever. Consciousness is tricky. To some it is awareness or finding our illusive "internal observer". Some call it "mindfulness". (Tashira Tachi-ren reportedly observed, "To gain the 95 percent of my brain that I haven't used, why did I have to lose the five percent I already had?") To others the task of consciousness is the healing of the soul. However conceived, what are we to be conscious of? Simply put, is it the true, rather than false self? That is difficult to know but if we truly recognize who we are, warts and all, as opposed to our ego ideal, we are less likely to engage the madness of the games. I have seen many people who sincerely believe they have changed and to a certain extent it may be true. Often, however, they have simply made a more functional adaptation and their level of consciousness remains unchanged. Expectations rather than acceptance remain at the core of their being.

In summary, if we want intimacy and serenity in our lives we must drop expectations and false hopes and surrender to acceptance, forgiveness, attentive listening, fair fighting, etc. We must have a willingness to engage in honesty rather than blaming or shaming. It is to accept responsibility including the ability to respond appropriately. We must be willing to give and to receive with gratitude, to pardon the other, to claim a repose or composure that strengthens the self and opens the way to responses from the heart rather than the head.

III   Intimacy, Love and Hate

Intimacy and love are often used synonymously. To be in love, to be with our beloved, to open one's heart to another is considered intimate. However, one can be intimately engaged with another out of feelings that are just the opposite. "Intimate enemies" has not been an uncommon term because of the ultimate concern about the "other". When the Cheka, the Tsarist secret police, followed Leon Trotsky in Paris, police documents held by the Hoover Institute at Stanford University indicate minute by minute, hour by day by month, all of Trotsky's movements, associates, living space, down to the public urinals he used when out of his flat. Super-sleuth spying left nothing private in one's life and privacy, too, is something we associate with intimacy. The intimate connection between enemies in the cold war even had unwritten rules of conduct, particularly in "wet cases" (assassinations) where tit equaled tat. There were few rules in trying for advantage over the other. **Trust**, another characteristic of intimacy, had meaning only in the sense of the prevailing unwritten rules. If one side could infiltrate the most closed sectors of the other's decision-making apparatus, it was fair game and to the victor went the spoils.

Intimate enemies also made the line between patriots and traitors very narrow. Vigilantism in the McCarthy era became excessive. Public privacy was violated by notions that, "only those who have something to hide are the ones who hide". To be an enemy of the state in the Soviet Union meant a Gulag in Siberia. Love and hate become blurred by ideas that you must do unto them as you believe they are doing unto you. Being "correct" is a feather in a high wind. The "passionate pursuit" of truth has as many psychopaths as it has men of God, both justifying their actions as "caring, loving and in the public interest".

In personal relationships we also find the difference between love and hate, loving connection and violation, a razor's edge almost as though borderline personalities were engaged with each other. In DSM IV the borderline is described as a person who makes a frantic effort to avoid abandonment and characteristically engages in inappropriate anger. All their relationships are intense and unstable. They idealize and then devalue, feeling the other person does not care enough, is not "there" enough, particularly when it comes to meeting their own needs. They are alternately beneficent and cruelly punitive. They may display extreme sarcasm, enduring bitterness, or simply verbal outbursts.

In abusive relationships, the beginnings may be "good", but there is a cycle of violence that is progressive. Unless stopped by a re-learning process by both parties, it leads to disaster, pain and ultimately physical injury. Remorse is only a temporary condition. At least one person has to "drop" and not give into or engage in greater or malicious conflict. A "drop" is like a time-out, a removal from the scene, and unwillingness to play the familiar pattern over and over. Participants in re-learning programs may be asked to re-enact the scenes of violence in slow motion (like in a movie) to discover where their decision points were; to recognize where they lost control; and to discover what other alternatives might have been possible in the situation. It takes considerable repetition for new behavior to emerge. Men often begin such programs with the assumption that they were "provoked" and women with the assumption that they are "innocent" of any wrong doings. Both may be correct but yet, in the end, they are false. In any case, why buy into provocation? Innocence is the avoidance of responsibility. Who really suffers in this playing out of love and hate? Both, but in the case of families, it is the children who later in life often repeat the same patterns.

Abuse may be the extreme in love/hate confusion but it is more common that one would like to think. It is estimated that two out of five women in the United States at one time or another have been victims of physical abuse. Child abuse is also a correlate. In New Zealand, for example, it is estimated that three out of five persons have been victims of child abuse.

To correct the sharp line between love and hate there has to be a program of "fair fighting" where rules do exist and the inevitable conflicts arising from just relating are managed in a constructive and healthy way. Without such rules of conduct such as, "no hitting below the belt", love and intimacy do not exist and we get the condition of intimate enemies.

Intimate enemies always suffer from terminal uniqueness in their "me-ness". In healthy intimacy, couples (or nations) know how to be close and still let the winds of heaven blow and dance between them without warfare.

IV   Intimacy and Sexuality

Why do we call the sexual act of intercourse intimate? Most of the reasons professed are merely reflections of traditional values, often prudish and irrelevant, hedonistic and superficial. Certainly the act of creation could be considered intimate by definition. But why is sex otherwise intimate? Primarily, it has been associated with sin, secrecy, desire, and lust in the interpretations of religionists, whether Christian or Moslem. A corollary of this is a devaluing of the "body-me", and speaks to the "higher nature of man", while sexuality speaks to his base instincts. Religionists have portrayed man's sin as carnal while Freud saw the ego and superego as functioning to control the id and its libidinal strivings. Freud's reality principle is a check on the pleasure principle. Without controls (according to the religionists and Freud) man might run amuck! Arguments from religion and science join.

The intimacy of sex in traditional negative notions connotes something private, sacred only to legitimate relations (i.e., marriage), and intensely personal. The sexual revolution of the 1960's made a mockery of traditional sexual values, upsetting to the point of violence for those considering themselves the protectors of morality and the family. Homosexuality could not be an intimate relationship because it was "unnatural". Abortion was a blow to the confinement of sexuality to the role of procreation. Thus sexuality and intimacy even became linked to murder, in some instances leading to arguments for the justifiable killing of doctors performing abortions. In these bizarre aberrations of twisted minds, sex and intimacy were ignored and irrelevant. Love and sex could be equated with justifiable homicide, bombings of abortion clinics, and flaunting of the law! The irony of preaching family values and practicing violent anarchy takes reason beyond the breaking point.

Nevertheless, there are at least three different views of the relationship between sex and intimacy. They may be summarized as follows:
(1)   I establish intimacy through the expression of my sexuality;
(2)   I express my sexuality after the establishment of intimacy; and

(3)   my sexuality and intimacy develop simultaneously for they are inter-
twined and inseparable with no first principle.

In the first view, sexuality is viewed as "experience near" and intimacy as
"experience distant". In the second case, it is just the opposite. The third
is the logical and rational approach but perhaps, in fact, the less frequent. I
shall conclude this section with a brief synopsis of "coupleship".

The first position is illustrated in the words of a 46-year-old divorcee
who has been through numerous short and long-term relationships.

> "A sexual relationship for me is a whole relationship – it is the way my longing
> for connection is expressed. It is a whole body, mind, emotional and spiritual
> experience. It grounds me in a relationship with the other because it grounds
> me in being a woman. Much of my child's distrust and mind trips are resolved
> when the sexual connection happens, for my child feels the woman connected
> to the other, and with that primal relationship in place, she feels secure."

While these eloquent words have a certain persuasive quality, the need to ground
in the other, the need to have her child's distrust resolved by the other, is indeed
primal as in "primary need". But it is also the voice of a dependent personality,
a voice saying to the other, "you will make me feel like a woman". It is neither
the voice of mature sexuality nor of intimacy. It is the voice calling for the lover
to fulfill her, to make her whole, to bring about a state of being.

The second position is illustrated by the thoughts of a 50-year-old professional man who has been married three times and despondent of finding
"the woman".

> "When I was younger, fucking was sport. Now I don't want to hop into bed
> with just anyone. After three marriages, one of which I felt was good, I want
> and need more. I don't 'perform' anymore and I have to establish at least a solid
> friendship before sex can be in any way fulfilling. Sex too early on, confuses
> me because I no longer know what it expresses."

In this statement there is caution and fear, perhaps realistic given the history. But there is also a withholding, a sense that, "I don't want to be hurt

again". Perhaps also, there is a wish for a guarantee before he can fully open to another, and of course no one can give such a promise.

In both of these first two positions the heart is withheld but for different reasons – "make me a woman", and "prove to me you love me". Both are probably bound for disappointment in their relationships because they exist at a superficial level. The "other" becomes the power broker in the relationship. They will go from partner to partner alternating between "over-giving" and "over-taking", with predictable dissatisfaction either on their part or the part of their potential mate.

Closely related to these approaches to intimacy and sexuality is the relationship between independence and dependence. One result of the woman's movement was to create confusion between the two, thereby seriously affecting the nature of intimate connections. In the rhetoric of the movement there seemed to be double messages such as, "I want to be close to you but also want my independence". In effect, women often wanted it both ways and on their own terms! They created a paradigm of paradox. Compliant as well as angry men, who now had lost their patriarchal role, did not how what to do and became weaker and weaker, for without that role an identity was lost without a clear replacement. Betty, a 35-year-old woman whose children were fast moving away from home, illustrates the woman's point of view and ensuing dilemma. She was losing her role as mother and although she was developing a solid professional life, she saw herself as a mother/wife with no identity other than that. To grow and extricate herself, she divorced in order to "find herself", to be for the first time in her life her own person, independent of relying on Dan, her ex-husband, to "take care of things". It was a radical solution to working out the balance between independence and dependence. While able to do so for a number of years, always feeling that Dan would be there when needed, she eventually re-married a man who she could dominate, as she felt she had been dominated by her father and by Dan. But in this process she lost a certain amount of her connection to intimacy as she slipped into "me-ness". She substituted professional achievement and security for the closeness that she wanted and for awhile seemed to shut down her heart. Slowly in her new relationship she began to rebuild.

Fundamental to all of this is the meaning of gender identity. With the sexual revolution, the woman's movement, and changes in traditional roles, the answer (beyond biology) of what it means to be a "man" or "woman" is unclear. Particularly for men there is no model except what they learned often times from absent father, peers, and cultural stereotypes. Robert Bly and James Hillman among many others have fervently addressed these problems and sought to raise the consciousness of men. For them self-expression is part of finding a vision. Yet our cultures persist with confusing notions of gender identity often leading to profound personal confusion.

Consider the case of Bob, a 55 year old successful business man. Bob's persona is that of a man's man. Underneath there is another story.

"Father was not there for me and he used alcohol to cover his woundedness and I had to be there, and wanted to be there for him. I didn't have any options. The feelings in me were intense and over-powering. There was a role reversal. I had to father my father in the hope that I could restore him in order to be his son. I had a strong realization of the 'wounded boy' in my father, and how he drank to avoid his pain. I realized how powerful and inter-generational this was on my male side as my grandfather was also a wounded person who drank.

There was an incident recently with a close friend who had several drinks one night and I remembered it all. The thoughts and feelings were that I wanted to offer my body to him to fuck. I wanted to go to his bed and somehow offer myself completely so he could be consoled and restored from his desperation. I wanted to be his 'wife' so that he could be whole. I was prepared to sacrifice everything so that then he could offer me a way out of my trap. I realized that by trying to restore my father to his masculinity I avoid my rage at his failure to have a strong heart and sexuality, to show me how to be a man and thereby save me from the castrating bitches. By being passive and 'wifely' with my sexuality I avoided the oedipal issue and avoid confronting the issue with my wife. She has my balls. By trying to restore his heart, I avoid my own broken heart and despair."

This small vignette raises the question of how does anyone become secure in his or her gender identity when there are few norms or inadequate models by which to evaluate it. Thus I wonder whether we are entering some kind of androgynous or confused age where culture and biology have not attained harmony?

The third position that sex and intimacy develop simultaneously is difficult to illustrate because it is not a condition often seen in the consulting room. People who have a "present heart" are able to clear the way in allowing their expression of self to deepen, to correspond to the other and to realize a "fulfillment", however illusive that term might seem. Their sexual relationship revolves around pleasure, in whatever exciting forms they choose or discover. They become partners in a voyage of total discovery. Sharon Wegscheider-Cruse summarizes characteristics of such "Coupleship":

➤ Have an outlook that is a couple's orientation toward shared experience.
➤ Give each other full and honest information.
➤ Trust each other.
➤ Take responsibility for self and are responsible to each other.
➤ Are loyally devoted to the other and have eliminated jealousy from their partnership.
➤ Are assertive, without being obnoxious, sarcastic and aggressive.
➤ Know how to fight fair and frequently.
➤ Are very affectionate.
➤ Are self and other accepting.
➤ Know how to discern what is important and what isn't.
➤ Have a sense of humor.
➤ Stick together in the hard or down times.
➤ Know how to play and laugh together.
➤ Are sexual with each other and maintain a sexually exclusive relationship.
➤ Know how to pray together.

Certainly the relationship between intimacy and sexuality has many complicated dimensions and one need not agree with the above characterization. Yet it is suggestive that a healthy relationship is a total participation in intimate connections. It is present oriented rather than being trapped in, say, the tyranny of the past.

I think the common denominator in sexuality and intimacy is the extent to which the heart is involved. One can have sex without intimacy and intimacy without sex. When they are combined in heart feelings, the power of each is doubled and a synergy developed as a new creation. The intimacy of sex is unique when it is an integration of body, mind, emotions and spirit. Soul as Eros and Eros as Soul!

V   Intimacy and Psychotherapy

By its very nature, psychotherapy is an intimate endeavor as two subjectivities work out a relationship, in the name of helping the one called, client. They create a reality between them that has all the aspects of intimacy already mentioned, minus sexual contact and the therapist revealing himself as would personal friends. The therapist works within the bounds of professional ethics and responsibility. It is the therapist's responsibility to protect boundaries and yet to encourage the client to go into himself in a deep and thorough way, to understand his own dynamics and change them if he so desires. The therapist may guide from time to time but more often is simply a partner on the journey of self-discovery. Rather than some, "behind the couch" neutrality, the therapist is there as a "real person" supporting insight rather than giving directives or making evaluations. Nevertheless, we must recognize the split among therapists regarding this approach. James Masterston argues that the therapist must be absolutely neutral, whereas Carl Rogers argued for a more positive identification with the client's process. The use of counter-transference is now a large issue in psychotherapy, particularly around early developmental issues.

In therapy a client literally spills his guts. This, among other things, leads to both love and hate of the therapist. Without an attuned and empathetic response from the therapist, the therapy will fail. The client's awareness and understanding may be a first time experience and thus will provoke many reactions. In seeing his own transference he will also be acutely aware of the counter-transference received from the therapist, however camouflaged the therapist may feel he is. Eventually, they stand rather naked before one another. Theirs is an intimate connection of soul meeting soul, the place where healing takes place.

Psychotherapy has elements of the intimacy of the confessional, but, except for certain types of behavioral therapy, there is no absolution. Instead there is interplay of dialectics recognizing the polarities in life. Therapy seeks to empower the individual to make choices, accept the consequences, and to function as part of a larger interdependence. The soul to soul contact with the therapist is to bring the person into the present rather than being mired in the past or futurizing. Being present also means dropping agendas represented, for example, by expectations or obsessions.

Therapy is a **reparative task** and as long as the "blocks" from the past are in full operation, neither therapist or client can succeed in their roles. To be a whole person, one needs to resolve the issues restricting personal integrity and have a zest for living in a complicated and often pessimistic world. Walking the line between pleasure and reality is not an easy task for anyone, including the therapist.

Where therapy falls short as an intimate connection is in adherence to a pathological model. The assumption of disturbance creates an atmosphere, which negates intimacy or the searching of two partners. Correcting pathology supersedes spiritual growth. The "me doctor", "you patient", removes an element of compassion or humanness from the scene. Assuming that the therapist is the expert in the human condition effectively puts the client in a one-down position and distorts the reality of his experience. Both the therapist and the client must enter the realms of mystery and paradox as partners. Interventions by the therapist follow the client's lead, not the opposite. The therapist is not some wizard, but if he really believes he has answers then he does come from Oz, and not all emotional problems can be reduced to a sexual etiology.

This is, however, a time of transition in psychotherapy. The traditional intimacy of the therapeutic relationship is in considerable jeopardy because of managed care, impositions by insurance companies, malpractice suits, the lack of concern about public health, etc. These developments are beyond the scope of this essay but the reader can find an excellent analysis in Lawrence E. Hedges, Robert Hilton, Virginia W. Hilton and O. Brandt Caudill Jr., <u>Therapists At Risk: Perils Of The Intimacy Of The Therapeutic Relationship</u>.

VI   Ego Psychology and Intimacy

The earth is an organism just as are our bodies. We either live in harmony or else we destroy it and ourselves at the same time. If Freud was basically right about persons having a "death wish", he was certainly right on a global scale. Instead of a sacred and intimate trust to preserve and protect the earth, man's total record is largely one of destruction, pillage and rape. Theodore Roszack asks the question, "Can the earth afford us?", if we do not live in intimacy and harmony with it? Can we respect the limits of the environments? Man's belief in the endless frontier is a psychotic dream.

I could present statistic after statistic concerning the destruction going on around us but what would be the point? The more pertinent question is about our beliefs and attitudes. Even in "green" New Zealand the sunburn warnings can get down to as little as three minutes because of the hole in the ozone layer in the Antarctic. And yet, this is a country that does not require catalytic converters in automobiles, thanks to the influence of the Petroleum industry. The incidence of melanoma there and in Australia has shown dramatic increases. Perhaps not until people are dying daily will there be a concentrated concern! How sad it is.

We live not in intimacy and harmony with the earth. Like the barbarians of old we seek to conquer rather than accept the damage we create. And if you have ever been to Bangkok or Sao Paulo you can see and feel what an inordinate disaster people can make out of a "city". "City Pox" is a yet another symptom. We still live with the positivist notion of "progress", celebrating man's arrogance to the peril of us all.

VII   Conclusion

Intimacy is a sacred trust, which has the quality of Grace-the incarnation of love, compassion and empathy. To be realized, it demands knowing our souls and a willingness to express that in our relationships and to the world as a whole. In that case we are never alone and we have the power to create, perhaps even a sane and sensible existence.

Introduction to Abstracts (in 6 languages)

Abstract Translations

A new feature in the IIBA Clinical Journal will be translations of the abstracts or summaries of the academic papers into five languages in addition to English. Below you will find abstracts of three original papers. We provide this service in consideration of those IIBA members who cannot read the articles in English. We hope to broaden the reading audience, and in so doing, honor the spirit of being a truly international community. We also hope the translated abstracts may lead groups to provide translation of the whole article for distribution.

Vincentia Schroeter

Übersetzung der Zusammenfassungen (German)

Neu ist in der Klinischen Zeitschrift des IIBA, dass die Zusammenfassungen der wissenschaftlichen Artikel neben Englisch in fünf weitere Sprachen übersetzt werden. Nachstehend finden Sie die Zusammenfassungen von drei Originalbeiträgen. Wir bieten diesen Dienst für IIBA-Mitglieder an, die die englischen Artikel nicht lesen können. Damit hoffen wir, unsere Leserschaft zu vergrößern und dem Geist einer wahrhaft internationalen Gemeinschaft zu dienen. Wir hoffen außerdem, dass die übersetzten Zusammenfassungen einzelne Gruppierungen dazu anregen wird, Übersetzungen ganzer Artikel zur weiteren Verteilung zu veranlassen.

Vincentia Schroeter (translated by Margit Koemeda)

Traductions de Resume (French)

Une nouveauté dans le Journal Clinique de l'IIBA va être la traduction des résumés des articles académiques en cinq langues en plus de l'anglais. Vous trouverez ci-dessous les résumés de trois articles nouveaux. Nous offrons ce service sachant que certains de nos membres ne comprennent pas l'anglais. Nous espérons élargir le nombre de lecteurs, et cela faisant, honorer l'esprit d'une vraie communauté internationale. Nous espérons également que ces résumés traduits puissent amener les groupes à offrir la traduction de l'ensemble de l'article pour distribution.

Vincentia Schroeter (translated by France Kauffmann)

Traducciones de Resúmenes (Spanish)

Una nueva característica de la Revista Clínica del IIBA será la traducción de los resúmenes de los artículos a cinco idiomas además del inglés.Debajo encontrareis los resúmenes de tres artículos.Ofrecemos este servicio en consideración a los miembros del IIBA que no pueden leer los artículos en inglés.Esperamos ampliar el público lector y al hacerlo honrar el espíritu de ser una verdadera comunidad internacional.Tambien albergamos la esperanza de que los resúmenes traducidos puedan propiciar que distintos grupos puedan proveer la traducción del artículo completo para su distribución.

Vincentia Schroeter (translated by Fina Pla)

Traduzione degli abstract (Italian)

Un nuovo servizio della rivista dell'Iiba saranno le traduzioni degli abstract o dei riassunti dei saggi in cinque lingue oltre l'inglese. Di seguito troverete gli abstract di tre articoli originali. Forniamo questo servizio in considerazione del fatto che non tutti i soci dell'Iiba sono in grado di leggere gli articoli in inglese. Ci auguriamo di far crescere il numero dei lettori, e facendo ciò, onorare lo spirito di essere una vera comunità internazionale. Ci auguriamo anche che gli abstract tradotti possano stimolare alla traduzione e alla diffusione dell'intero articolo.

Vincentia Schroeter (translated by Rosaria Filoni)

Traduções de Resumos (Portuguese)

Uma novidade que o periódico do IIBA irá oferecer será a publicação dos resumos e sumários de dissertações acadêmicas, agora traduzidos para cinco línguas, além do inglês. Abaixo vocês encontrarão resumos de três dissertações originais. Nós estamos provendo este serviço em consideração a aqueles membros do IIBA que não conseguem ler os artigos em inglês. Desejamos que desta forma o público leitor cresça, e desta forma, possamos honrar o espírito de ser uma verdadeira comunidade internacional. Também temos esperança de que os resumos traduzidos motivem alguns grupos a oferecerem traduções para o artigo completo, para que assim possamos fazer sua distribuição.

Vincentia Schroeter (translated by Camile Milagres)

Trusting the Wisdom of the Failing Body[1]

From Well-Being to Illness: A Journey towards Wholeness

Louise Fréchette

Abstracts

English

Through research data and clinical vignettes, this article analyzes the question of physical illness within the paradigm of a personal development process. It argues that physical illness should not be interpreted as a failure to live up to our Bioenergetic Analysis values and principles. Instead, physical illness can be viewed as an integral part of a person's personal growth journey; as a manifestation of guidance from our organism; and as an attempt from our body to steer us towards a path that may lead to deeper emotional and spiritual healing.

---

1 Presentation given at the Southern California Bioenergetic Conference; Lake Arrowhead, March 13–16, 2009.

Der Weisheit des versagenden Körpers vertrauen. Von der Gesundheit zur Krankheit: Eine Reise zur Ganzheit (German)

Auf der Grundlage von Forschungsergebnissen und Fallvignetten wird in diesem Beitrag körperliche Krankheit unter der Leitidee von persönlichen Entwicklungsprozessen untersucht. Körperliche Krankheit sollte nicht als Versagen betrachtet werden, unseren bioenergetisch-analytischen Idealen und Prinzipien zu genügen. Stattdessen kann körperliche Krankheit als unverzichtbarer Teil persönlichen Wachstums aufgefasst werden; als Manifestation des Umstandes, dass der Organismus die Führung übernimmt; als Versuch unseres Körpers, uns auf einen Pfad zu bringen, der zu einer tieferen emotionalen und geistigen Heilung führt.

Faire confiance à la sagesse du corps qui nous lâche. Passer de la santé à la maladie: un voyage initiatique vers l'unification de soi (French)

À l'aide de données fournies par la recherche de même que de quelques vignettes cliniques, cet article analyse la question des problèmes de santé physique dans la perspective d'un processus de développement personnel. Il tente d'expliquer en quoi la maladie ne devrait pas être interprétée comme étant un échec en regard de notre capacité à incarner les valeurs et les principes de l'analyse bioénergétique. Elle peut au contraire être vue comme faisant partie intégrante du cheminement de développement personnel de tout être, comme une forme de communication de notre organisme, une tentative de notre corps destinée à nous orienter vers une guérison profonde tant au plan émotionnel que spirituel.

Confiando en la sabiduria de los puntos débiles del cuerpo. De la salud a la enfermedad: Un viaje hacia la completitud (Spanish)

A partir de datos de investigación y casos clínicos, este artículo analiza la cuestión de la enfermedad física desde la perspectiva del proceso de desarrollo personal. Argumenta que la enfermedad física no debería ser interpretada necesariamente como un fracaso, si nos basamos en los valores y principios del análisis bioenergético. En cambio, podemos verla como parte integrante del camino de desarrollo personal del sujeto, como una comunicación orientativa de nuestro organismo, un intento por parte de nuestro cuerpo de guiarnos por una senda que lleve a una curación tanto emocional como espiritual más profunda.

Avere fiducia nella saggezza del corpo che ci abbandona. Dal benessere alla malattia: un viaggio iniziatico verso l'integrazione del Sé (Italiano)

Grazie ai risultati della ricerca e a vignette cliniche, questo articolo analizza il tema dei problemi di salute fisica nella prospettiva di un processo di sviluppo personale. Si propone di spiegare che la malattia fisica non va interpretata come un fallimento della nostra capacità di incarnare i valori e principi dell'analisi bioenergetica. Al contrario, la malattia fisica può essere considerata parte integrante del soggettivo percorso di crescita personale, come una forma di comunicazione del nostro organismo, un tentativo del nostro corpo di orientarci verso una guarigione profonda sia sul piano emotivo che spirituale.

Confiando na sabedoria do Corpo em Crise. Do bem estar para a doença: Uma jornada em direção à integração (Português)

A partir de dados de pesquisa e casos clínicos, este artigo analisa a questão da doença física desde a perspectiva do processo de desenvolvimento pessoal. Argumenta que a doença física não deve ser interpretada como um fracasso por não se ter conseguido viver de acordo com os valores e princípios da Análise Bioenergética. Ao invés disso, pode ser vista enquanto parte integrante da jornada de desenvolvimento pessoal, enquanto uma manifestação orientadora do nosso organismo, e enquanto uma tentativa do nosso corpo de nos impelir na direção de um caminho que poderá levar a uma cura emocional e espiritual mais profunda.

Trusting the Wisdom of the Failing Body – From Well-being to Illness: A Journey towards Wholeness

If I chose to present on the topic of the wisdom of the failing body, it is because, although we rarely see the failing body as a blessing, it can teach us profound lessons about how we live our lives. It is also because, as Bioenergetic therapists, we are bound to develop an interest in psychosomatic problems, especially since our clients come to us not only with their emotional problems, but often times with somatic problems as well.

As we know, Bioenergetic Analysis is a wonderful approach designed to help us understand the complex interaction between body and psyche. The theoretical foundation on which Bioenergetic Analysis is elaborated, gives us a model of physical and mental health, whereby an individual should ideally be relatively free of tension so that energy flows freely from the core to the periphery of the organism. This enables the individual to be expressive and grounded in reality, as well as in adult sexuality. Alexander Lowen explains it thus:

"Let us assume for the purpose of the discussion that it is possible to eliminate every defensive position in the personality. How would **a healthy person** function? What would our diagram look like?

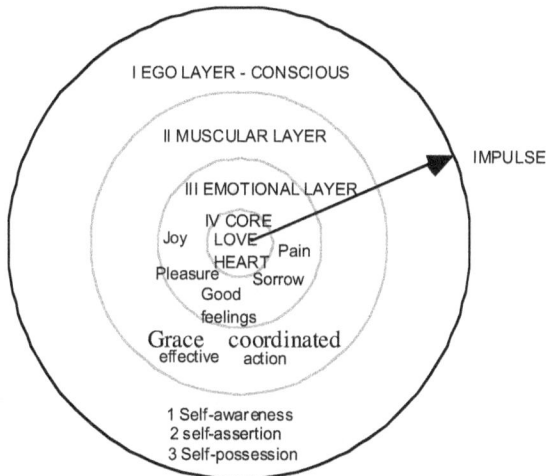

Figure 1: Coordinating and expressive layers in a healthy person (Lowen, Bioenergetics, p. 123)

– all impulses would flow from the heart,
– he would also respond emotionally in all situations:
– his actions and movements would be graceful and effective.
The basic quality of the person would be one of ease as opposed to dis-ease; his basic mood would be one of well-being. He would be joyful or sorrowful as circumstances dictated, but in all his responses he would be a healthy person" (**Lowen**, *Bioenergetics*, pp. 123–124).

Although we all know that the model **Alexander Lowen** describes is a utopian model, deep down inside, we nevertheless tend to use it as the gold standard by which we measure our own success as psychotherapists and as individuals. Given that, it is easy for Bioenergetic therapists to feel ashamed if we fail to help a client heal, or at least reduce the client's psychosomatic symptoms. It can be even more shameful if we ourselves are diagnosed with some kind of physical illness, or if we develop chronic ailments.

I do not want to challenge the presumption that physical illnesses or problems may reflect unresolved psychological issues. I believe that most of the time they do, at least to some degree. However, I would like to challenge the implicit belief that physical illnesses or physical problems should be equated with psychotherapeutic failure. I would like to reframe physical illness or problems as being part of a self-developmental process, something we should not be ashamed of, but rather, something we should welcome as a signpost along the way, to help us find the right direction in our quest for wholeness. I propose that we can transform the sense of failure we may experience when the body fails us, into a sense of wonder that such a complex organism should attempt to communicate, in its own language, something of vital importance to us.

When the Body Fails Us: from Small Failures to Severe Failures

We can view the theme of the failing body in a way that refers to mild as well as more severe types of physical illnesses. It is not my intention to give tips on how to deal with the specifics of various health conditions. Rather, in this article I want to reflect on the question of physical illness in our clinical work with clients, as well as in our daily lives when we ourselves are faced with our own illness. I will highlight the factors that can cause physical illness. I will also share a few clinical vignettes that may help us understand the kind of strategies, as well as the kind of attitudes we can develop to cope with the unexpected when, suddenly, the body doesn't respond as well as it used to; when it fails our clients; or when it fails us.

The Body-Psyche Connection in the Case of Physical Illness: a brief look at the Evolution of the Concept

For psychotherapists, and even more so for us, Bioenergetic therapists, it has been clear for a long time that there is a connection between physical problems and the psychological patterns of a client. We understand that there is a need to work through emotional issues in order to promote physical healing as well as psychological healing. This understanding is not altogether new.

Freud recognized the relationship between hysterical repression and somatic symptoms. One of Freud's contemporaries, Georg Groddeck, a German physician, would look for emotionally traumatic events that could have triggered a particular physical illness in his patients. Groddeck looked for this connection as early as 1917. A few years later, Reich also speculated about the psychic nature of certain physical illnesses, and connected cancer with an attitude of emotional resignation. In 1935, Helen Flanders Dunbar, an American woman from Chicago, (with degrees in mathematics, psychology, philosophy and theology), published a book entitled, *Emotions and Bodily Changes*. She postulated that certain personality types are more prone to certain physical illnesses. A few decades later, during the 1950's, came the famous study by Meyer Friedman and Ray Rosenman, demonstrating that hyperactive, extrovert, Type A personalities were more apt to suffer from cardiovascular problems, while introvert and externally calm, Type C personalities were more prone to autoimmune diseases. Type B personalities, on the other hand, were seen as more balanced and therefore less likely to suffer from problems of physical health.

Lowen himself, back in 1980, wrote an article entitled, *Stress and Illness: A Bioenergetic View*, in which he offers various hypotheses with regard to physical illnesses such as tuberculosis, cancer, arthritis, heart attack and ulcerative colitis. Later, he published *Love, Sex and Your Heart*, a book devoted to the analysis of the emotional underpinnings of cardiac problems.

Since then, countless studies and theoretical essays have been published on the subject, while new studies continue to be conducted. There are studies on the impact of positive feelings on a person's physical health. Some of these are being conducted at the **HeartMath Institute,** where ECG patterns are recorded and compared to positive or negative emotional states and their impact on body cells. Various studies are being conducted at the Virginia Commonwealth University by **Dr. Everett Worthington,** which are on the impact of forgiveness on a person's physical well-being. **Professor Carol Ryff,** is making other studies at the University of Wisconsin, with respect to the relationship between psychological well-being and neurobiology. Professor Ryff studies the impact of emotional well-being on neural circuitry, neuroendocrine regulation, inflammatory processes, cardiovascular risk, as well as on the general resilience of the organism. **Ernest Rossi,** a disciple of the great hypnotherapist, **Milton Erickson,** has written several books on the topic of mind-body communication during hypnotic states. In one of his books, entitled, *The Symptom Path to Enlightenment,* **Rossi** devotes a whole chapter to *The Neuroendocrine Information Loop Between Brain and Body.* He explains that substances called 'molecular messengers' or 'informational substances', are believed to,

> "modulate the action of neurons and cells at all levels from the basic pathways of sensation and perception to the regulation of the homeostatic processes of life on the molecular-genetic-cellular levels."[2]

Reading this chapter certainly leaves one in awe of the complexity and sophistication by which information travels in our organism. Then there are **Antonio Damasio's** findings that demonstrate that, "emotions are brain representations of body states." Finally, **Allan Schore,** another prominent researcher in this field, explains how the quality of primary human interaction, at the very beginning of life, can affect one's capacity to self-regulate later, both emotionally and somatically.

Clearly, the psychological, endocrinological and neurological fields are coming together and are closing the gap between the mind-body dichotomy that our Judeo-Christian tradition taught us, had existed for so long.

---

2 E. Rossi, The Symptom Path to Enlightenment, pp. 96–97

When the Body Screams, "Help!"

The body is a marvelous and extraordinarily complex organism that has accumulated the wisdom of billions of years of evolution, since life first started on this planet. We are just beginning to unveil the workings of some of its deepest mysteries through research on how DNA carries the blueprint for so many vital functions. When we think of it, it is a miracle that our body does not fail us any more than it does. And when it does, it is because its incredible adaptive mechanisms can no longer cope with the state of imbalance it is submitted to. Along with a state of imbalance, our poor capacity to self-regulate; as well as the lack of communication between the various somatic components; contribute to weaken our body's adaptive mechanisms and pave the way to physical illness. We will now examine more closely what pushes that marvelously complex and ingenious organism over the edge, causing it to fail us.

Ideally, being and feeling physically and emotionally healthy is related to a state of balance. In Bioenergetic terms, this means that one is in a state of free flowing energy, from head to toe, from center to periphery, just as we saw in **Lowen's** diagram at the beginning of this presentation. One experiences a rhythmic, pulsative activity in one's organism, as described by **Reich** and by **Keleman**. This goes along with a good capacity to sense, to express and to assert oneself in the world.

However, life being what it is, there are few, if any, individuals that fit the ideal model. Because of our personal history, we have had to contract and defend ourselves in many ways in order to cope with the hardships of life. Fortunately, that incredible lifelong companion, that is our body, can draw on the wisdom of billions of years of evolution during which living organisms evolved. So, built into our very cells are many adaptive resources that can aptly manage, for a while, a relatively good range of states of imbalance, before breaking down and "failing" us, so to speak.

State of Imbalance as a Factor that May Precipitate Physical illness

What are we talking about, when we talk about states of imbalance? Basically, we are talking about situations where the level of stress is such that it exceeds our capacity to manage it, and so this is the point where the scales are tipped. What are those situations? We will consult the well-known stress scale designed forty years ago in 1967 by **Holmes** and **Rahe.** We see a list of situations that can induce a level of stress that challenges the organism's capacity to adapt and that may put a person at risk of physical illness (or accident). The life change units indicated beside each situation serve to tally a score that indicates the level of risk of physical illness. The tally takes into consideration **only events that have occurred in the past YEAR** of an individual's life.

Life event	Life change units	Life event	Life change units
Death of a spouse	100	Trouble with in-laws	29
Divorce	73	Outstanding personal achievement	28
Marital separation	65	Spouse starts or stops work	26
Imprisonment	63	Begin or end school	26
Death of a close family member	63	Change in living conditions	25
Personal injury or illness	53	Revision of personal habits	24
Marriage	50	Trouble with boss	23
Dismissal from work	47	Change in working hours or conditions	20
Marital reconciliation	45	Change in residence	20
Retirement	45	Change in schools	20
Change in health of family member	44	Change in recreation	19
Pregnancy	40	Change in church activities	19
Sexual difficulties	39	Change in social activities	18
Gain a new family member	39	Minor mortgage or loan	17
Business readjustment	39	Change in sleeping habits	16

Change in financial state	38	Change in number of family reunions	15
Change in frequency of arguments	35	Change in eating habits	15
Major mortgage	32	Vacation	13
Foreclosure of mortgage or loan	30	Christmas	12
Change in responsibilities at work	29	Minor violation of law	11
Child leaving home	29		

Score of 300+: At risk of physical illness.

Score of 150–299: Risk of physical illness is moderate (reduced by 30% from the above risk).

Score –150: Only have a slight risk of physical illness.

Although **Holmes** and **Rahe**'s stress scale is still relevant to some degree, one must acknowledge that the world has changed considerably since 1967. In the midst of a world that seems to come undone more and more every day, the individual faces a level of stress that demands a lot of the adaptive potential of the individual's organism. The capacity to maintain one's emotional and physical balance in that context is, to say the least, sorely challenged. But this is precisely the time, when it becomes important to listen to the wisdom of one's failing body, as it cries out, through the language of symptoms, to come back to the essence of a balanced, healthy life.

Poor Capacity to Self-regulate as another Factor that May Precipitate Physical Illness

Self-regulation refers to the capacity of the person to process and modulate somatic and emotional experience, so that the person will not be overwhelmed by it. In Bioenergetic Analysis, we often use the term 'containment' to describe that crucial function. **Allan Shore**, in his book, *Affect Regulation and the Origin of the Self*, explains how primary attachment patterns affect our brains, and consequently our basic organismic capacity to self-regulate throughout life.

When the primary caregivers are unable to offer a 'good enough' quality of attunement to the infant, later on the adult may have a poor capacity to self-regulate. This, in turn, may leave the organism more exposed to somatic problems. In an interesting book entitled, *Full Catastrophe Living: Using the Wisdom of Your Body and Mind to Face Stress, Pain and Illness*, **Dr. Jon Kabat-Zinn**, reports on numerous studies that demonstrate the role of emotions in physical health. One of these studies, on a group of women who were diagnosed with a lump in one of their breasts, clearly highlights the connection that exists between affect regulation (or lack of) and the risk for cancer. In the words of **Kabat-Zinn:**

> "The majority of women who were found to have breast cancer had either a lifelong pattern of extreme suppression of their feelings (for the most part anger) or of 'exploding' with emotion." (**Jon Kabat-Zinn**, *Full Catastrophe Living*, p. 207)

Of course, this is not new to Bioenergetic therapists, because we know a great deal about the importance of good energy circulation in the body. We also know the importance of being able to feel, contain and express emotions in a regulated way, in order to stay emotionally and physically healthy.

Learning to Self-regulate: a Case of Ulcerative Colitis

Not only do we know about these things, but we are also starting to write about them. In an interesting article published in 2007 in the *Clinical Journal of the IIBA*, **Jörg Clauer**, a German CBT and medical doctor, shares with the reader his clinical experience with a client who was suffering from ulcerative colitis and seasonal depression. **Clauer** explains that he basically worked with this client at reconstructing a new embodied self, and that in order for this to be accomplished, he had to apply the principle of the three S's: Slowness, Safety and Support. What guided him in his work was his embodied countertransference. **Shore's** findings in neurobiology, together with those of **D. N. Stern** and **K. Uvnaes-Möberg,** among others, turned out to be guidelines to explain the therapy process.

Given this understanding of the core issue of his client, **Clauer** proceeded to work with this client in such as way as to help her reconnect with her bodily sensations through various grounding exercises. He used a balance disk, so that she could learn to feel more at ease in her body and heal her dissociation or mind/body split. On the interpersonal level, he facilitated a dialog between the client and himself as a 'parent-body'. Having the client, for example, sitting back-to-back with him, helped her gain more self-awareness. Then came a phase when **Clauer** was going away for a vacation and would be missing an appointment. This triggered the client's feeling of abandonment and subsequent anger, as it was experienced as a repetition of her own history. The capacity of the client to then actively express her anger to the therapist marked a positive evolution in the therapy.

The whole process, according to **Clauer,** led to developing the Body Self and a New Implicit Relational Knowledge that led to Changes in the Mental-Organizing Principles. This means that the client's outlook on life and on her relationship with her parents was significantly modified by the dynamics of the interaction in the therapeutic experience. **Clauer** concludes his clinical vignette by saying: "To the amazement of the gastroenterologist, the colitis-changes were not any longer detectable at a post examining colonoscopy" (p. 118).

Lack of Communication within the Organism, a Third Factor that May Precipitate Physical illness

Communication in the form of exchange of information is vital for survival. Exchange of information is constantly at work in our organism. As explained by **Ernest Rossi,** the nervous system plays that crucial role (of exchange of information), through electric impulses, as do the endocrine and the immune systems through various substances such as hormones and proteins.

In Bioenergetic Analysis, we are aware of the importance of re-establishing pathways of communication in the body. When we propose exercises designed either to soften the muscular blocks or to call attention to inner body sensations, we intend to restore the flow of energy in the body. We are also aware that the creation of a safe space and the establishment of a safe interpersonal relationship, are crucial factors for bridging the gap between the psychic and the somatic worlds. This is especially true when trauma has brought about a fair degree of dissociation. In so doing, we are taking into consideration the impact of the infant's very early experiences on his or her capacity to cope with the stress of life later on.

Restoring Communication and Continuity within the Body: a Case of Cancer

One of our colleagues from the IIBA Faculty, **Guy Tonella**, is currently developing a very interesting theoretical model that combines concepts from attachment theory and from neuroscience with basic Bioenergetic Analysis concepts. In an instructive article titled, *Symptôme psychosomatique et intégration corporelle* (Psychosomatic Symptom and Psychosomatic Integration), **Tonella** reports on the therapeutic process of one of his clients, a young woman who came to him with a very serious health condition. She had been diagnosed with thymus cancer that had metastasized to her lungs, with the presence of nodules in the liver and in the uterus.

The client's doctor had told **Guy Tonella** that the client was terminally ill and had only a three to six months life expectancy. Nevertheless, **Tonella** began to work with her, clearly seeing right from the start the degree of lack of integration in this woman's body. Her mother had been mentally unstable and violent and her narcissistic father had been mainly absent. **Tonella** explains in this article how he worked subtly at the somatic-tonic level, that is to say beyond words, re-creating a safe bond that eventually allowed the client to reconnect with her primary, vital impulses, and to express emotions she had to split off from long ago. Throughout the therapeutic journey of this woman, **Tonella** consistently worked from an attuned position, using various holding techniques, sensitive touch, and interaction through eye contact. All of this eventually helped the client break down and sob deeply, and then, later on in the process, enabled her to express her anger through hitting. According to **Tonella**, it is this kind of work that allowed the restoration of continuity between the tonic, the sensory, the affective and the representational layers of the client's being. Towards the end of the therapy, as she was regaining a sensation of vitality, the client told **Tonella:**

> "I have the impression that I am discovering my movements, my true movements that help me feel good, movements that are in tune with me, in which I care for myself. I feel that I am really starting to love myself. I am beginning to love people without quite knowing yet how to relate to them. My fear of people is disappearing. And I love myself! I am beginning to feel good inside myself, even though I do not feel too good physically speaking."

When I discussed this article with **Guy Tonella,** he told me that his patient actually lived for a year and a half notwithstanding her doctor's prognosis that her life expectancy would probably not exceed 6 months. Not only that, and even more important, he helped her re-establish a sense of continuity between all the layers of her being. From the most primitive nucleus, that of the sensory-tonic sensations, to the more sophisticated functions, such as the representational one, **Guy** helped her regain a sense of herself and a sense of being alive that she could never have experienced otherwise.

Listening to the Wisdom of the Failing Body: Many Points of Entry, Many Paths towards Healing and Wholeness

From the clinical vignettes I just presented, we already see that various dimensions of the person are involved in the healing process. These various dimensions can be seen as points of entry from which to approach the problem when the body speaks its wisdom through its failure. First, there is the somatic layer, the body itself; then, there is the emotional layer, the domain of feelings; and finally there is the representational layer that is related to the mind, to the thought processes and to the symbolical realm.

As Bioenergetic therapists, we are equipped to propose various exercises that will help a person be in touch with the person's physical sensations. However, because we possess these tools, we may be tempted to work "from the outside in", so to speak, creating between us and the client a type of dynamic that will resemble that of the doctor/patient relationship, where one holds the knowledge while the other undergoes the treatment. This can go on at a very subtle level, especially when the client who comes to us is in a desperate place and seeks to be cured by us.

Out of a genuine desire to help the client get relief from suffering – and also because of our own narcissistic issues – we want to get positive results as soon as possible. So, on a verbal level we may explain to the client that psychotherapy is about him being involved as a major actor in his own process. Yet, on the interactional level, we may take charge of the process, unconsciously demanding of ourselves to have a quick grasp of the connection between the health condition of the client and the underlying emotional issues of the client. We will also expect ourselves to know the kind of energetic work the client needs to do, in order to improve the client's condition. And then, we will have created the perfect setup in which, not only will we overburden ourselves with a level of responsibility far beyond what it should be, but we will deprive the client of the opportunity to become the central actor in his own healing process.

So, as we approach the client's problem, both from a physical and an emotional angle, as we are trained to do, it becomes important to work "from the inside out". But what does that mean concretely? It means that we have to get our cues from the client's organic rhythm, and from the client's capacity to create solutions, rather than from our preconceived notions.

Working "From the Inside Out": coping with Fibromyalgia

Here is another clinical vignette to illustrate my point. A female client who came to see me many years ago for problems related to anger control, started to suffer from fibromyalgia in the course of her therapy. I worked with her for quite a while on issues related to the expression of anger, having her kick and scream and hit with a tennis racket, while also extensively working on grounding. I was operating under the assumption that if she could discharge her anger and gain a better understanding of it, not only would she develop a better capacity to contain and regulate her anger, but she would also get relief from her fibromyalgia symptoms. This strategy helped to some extent, but what helped even more was when I started to work with her, using what **Jörg Clauer** called, "the three S's": Slowness, Safety and Support. She came back to therapy last year to get some help around an issue of self-assertion at work. Instead of proposing various exercises, I would sit and listen to what she would tell me about her pain, inviting her to focus on her breathing. I followed the small and slow movements of her body and tried to attune my verbal interventions, as well as my body posture to hers; using techniques I had learned from my hypnosis training. At one point, I invited her to move through her body, to observe the rhythm of her breathing and to imagine she was finding a way to ease the pain in her joints. I encouraged her to focus on her inner resources. The image that came to her was that of two small hands moving inside her body, massaging a soothing substance on the painful spots. This client still copes with fibromyalgia, but 'the little hands', as she calls them, are still with her and continue to help her ease the pain in her body during periods of stress.

My point is that I mainly tried to establish a kind of somatic dialog with her body, coupled with an invitation to use her own resources of sensorial imagination, as opposed to trying to give an interpretation to her symptoms of fibromyalgia.

The 'inside out' approach demands of us that we become attentive and attuned to the natural signals the body is giving us, to its micro movements, taking advantage of the "three S's" approach: Slowness, Safety and Support. It also requires that we be humble and patient and that we trust the organic process of the client. This organic process can sometimes express itself through small and slow movements, as well as through intense and cathartic ones.

Emotional Expression and Healing: Coping with Gastrointestinal Problems

Regarding strategies that are geared towards the emotional point of entry that can promote healing, I recall another client of mine who came to me with symptoms of painful gastrointestinal problems as well as a problem of acute anxiety and low self-esteem. This client had grown up in a family of many brothers and sisters. Contrary to his brothers who excelled at sports, and who lived up to their father's expectations, he excelled neither at sports nor academically. He was physically smaller than his brothers and did not enjoy rough physical activities. When he reached secondary school, he decided he would work hard in order to succeed academically. He did, and went on eventually to complete a university degree. His father took no notice of his success, he never gave him any sort of encouragement, and he continued to treat him with contempt. Even though this client has a successful career, taking on positions that required leadership talent, he never managed to develop a feeling of self-worth. For several years he had been able to alleviate his symptoms through high caliber biking. This not only helped him discharge inner tension, but also helped him raise his self-esteem, because of his achievements in that sport.

When he came to see me, his gastrointestinal problems and his level of anxiety were on the rise, since knee and back problems prevented him from continuing his biking activities as intensely as he used to. Coming to therapy was a source of acute anxiety for him. It meant facing and revealing his own self, when he basically despised himself as his father had. In the course of a therapy session, he started to talk about the grief he felt at not having been acknowledged by his father and at the harshness with which his father had treated him. I encouraged him to listen to the wave of emotion that was coming from his gut and to share with me more of his history, and more of what he would have wanted to tell his father, had he been able to. He then started to sob deeply, as he continued to talk about how much he had felt like a failure when he would see that look in his father's eyes. At the end of the session, he felt a form of relief he had not been able to feel for a long time.

Subsequently, whenever he cried deeply during a session, he would feel the same relief and gradually his gastrointestinal problems subsided. They are altogether gone, because he still struggles with that symptom whenever he faces a stressful situation. But he is getting better at digging himself out of this hole of anxiety and self-loathing that he had been in for most of his life.

My understanding of what helped relieve the physical gastrointestinal symptom of this client is twofold. On the one hand, the sobbing certainly helped release the tension in the deep abdominal tissue, so that some kind of regulative process could be restored. On the other hand, for the first time in his life, this man willingly, 'broke down' emotionally, and courageously exposed his feelings of fear and hurt. This in itself implied that he acknowledged himself as worthy enough to cry out for help and ask to be cared for. As he learned to break down emotionally and cry for help, it seemed as though his body did not need to "scream" as much as it used to. As for the therapeutic strategy, I think that in this case, here is what was most helpful – in addition to the bodywork we had been doing. What was most helpful was my empathic listening, my not using too many words, my repeated encouragement to value his process, and my readiness to hear what he would share with me. I listened as the subjective experience of his pain emerged and took form and meaning through his own words.

Mindset, Beliefs and Attitudes that Promote Healing

Mindset, beliefs and attitudes are crucial factors that can affect our physical health as well. They also constitute a third point of entry with regards to healing strategies. **Dr. Jon Kabat-Zinn**, in his book, *Full Catastrophe Living*, reports on various studies that demonstrate that some basic perceptions and thought patterns can make a difference between health and physical illness. One of these patterns is that of *optimism vs. pessimism.* According to certain studies he cites, optimism appears to have "a protective effect against depression, illness and premature death" (p. 201). Then, there is *self-efficacy*, a belief in one's ability to exercise control over specific life events in one's life. This factor, according to another set of studies, "is the best and most consistent predictor of positive health outcomes in many different medical situations" (p. 201). Finally, he mentions the inherent *sense of coherence* about the world and oneself, which refers to one's capacity to give a meaning to a painful situation.

A certain number of scientific studies tell us about the positive impact of positive perceptions and thought patterns. However, these thought patterns cannot be developed merely through willpower. They need to evolve from a set of attitudes that can be cultivated. The fact is that all of us have some degree of choice. We can choose for the better, in spite of our character structure that operates quasi-automatically, or even on an unconscious level. But deliberately making choices, which lead to positive change, does not come easily. We often prefer to stay in a miserable condition that we are accustomed to, rather than risk stepping into the unknown. Consequently, we stick to our habits, good or bad, until something really disturbing, such as when our body fails us, forces us to change our patterns. **Jung** used to say: "Illness is an effort made by nature in order to cure us." And true enough; physical illness is a call from deep down inside, which beckons us to learn new ways of dealing with life's challenges in order to honor our true nature. And as we make the changes that enable us to get more in tune with who we truly are, and with our purpose in life, the body can start to heal.

Some people have to change careers in order to honor their deeper self, while others have to learn to set their limits in their workplace in order to stop energy drainage. Some have to learn to cry and soften their hearts, while others have to learn how to get angry and stand up for themselves. And some have to put an end to a relationship, while others have to learn to forgive their partners. Changes need to be made in order to recover our health, or to adapt to whatever limitations physical illness places upon us. The basic ingredients that should underlie all those changes are self-love and acceptance. We need to accept whatever life brings to us, and accept who we are, in the moment. Then, last but not least, we need faith, be it faith in one's capacity to heal oneself or in some superior power.

And even when a person does not heal completely, as in the case of my two clients, the rapport with oneself changes dramatically. Instead of feeling held hostage by one's physical condition, like a victim, the person can learn to take charge of her process, in a caring and compassionate way towards herself. She can begin to treat her own body like a wise companion, one that is trying to help her find a path towards wholeness.

When the body fails to heal

But then, what if, after having done our best to restore our health through energetic work, emotional work and work on our thought patterns and belief system, we are still not recovering? What if physical illness does not release its grip on us? What if physical illness slowly takes us down the road to our very end? Does that mean we have failed, or is it just another phase on the road in our personal journey towards self-realization and wholeness?

In an attempt to answer those questions, I would like to share with you the extraordinary journey of a student of mine. Emma[3] entered the BioenergeticTraining Program when she was in her mid-forties. She was a woman of incredible vitality – an outspoken, sensitive, vibrant woman and an extremely motivated participant. Emma and I shared a special moment when, in the course of the second or third workshop I had been giving, I did a piece of work with her that she experienced as life changing. Over the five years during which I did these workshops, I developed a strong

---

3 The names have been changed and certain details have been slightly altered in order to preserve confidentiality.

connection with Emma. We kept in touch from time to time, through email, after the completion of the fifth and last year of training.

I had gone several months without hearing from Emma when, during one of my trips to her country, I met with one of her fellow participants who told me that she had been diagnosed with mouth cancer, and was undergoing a series of treatments. This news had been shocking to Emma as she had very healthy life habits, had never smoked nor done anything that could be considered a risk factor for that kind of cancer. I could not believe this was happening to Emma. I reconnected with her through email. She shared some of her emotional experience with me, as she was going through all kinds of treatments, from conventional to alternative medicine. Emma wrote to me about the inner work she was actively doing. She was trying to understand the meaning of this awful type of cancer, accessing new emotional layers and trying to come to terms with her deepest issues, in the hope that emotional healing would bring somatic healing.

As the cancer evolved, Emma went through several major physical losses. After a while, she, who had been a woman who loved to savor life and especially enjoyed good food, lost the capacity to eat solid food. She had to be fed with liquid substances, thus having to let go of the pleasure of tasting and eating solid food. Then, she who had been so proud of her appearance, saw part of her jaw gradually destroyed by cancerous tissues, and had to grieve her good looks.

As Emma was going through all of this, she chose, paradoxically, to envision this process as a healing process on a spiritual level. She wrote to me some poignant reflexions on how life was stripping her of the superfluous to bring her to meet the essence of life and love. This is not to say that she never experienced fear, sorrow, anger, despair, especially as she saw part of her face literally disintegrate. However, the wholeheartedness with which she embraced her ordeal, while doing all that was in her power in order to cure herself, sometimes made me cry when I read her messages. Emma never gave up on hope, yet she completely surrendered to the somatic, emotional and spiritual process that was unfolding.

A week or so before she passed away, on the blog some of her friends had created for her, so that she could keep in touch with minimal effort with all of those who cared for her, Emma wrote:

"It is true that I have sowed many seeds throughout my life and to me, your love is a living proof of that. You truly are a path of flowers ... but I feel frustrated not to be able to find the path that could bring me back to a genuine and total love of myself. I would not want to die before I reach that stage. Because I truly believe that this is the path ... being able to love in such a way that each and every one of my cells feels loved."

Then, a few days later, Emma wrote again:

"Dear friends. Here I am again, at this wonderful window that the universe keeps open for us so that we can see the immensity of the stars, of the seas, of the deserts and of this river of love that we are creating ... it is such, such a beautiful view that which I see from here, that it absorbs me and I am transforming into that which I am looking at: a star, a wave, a grain of sand ... the pure essence of love.

May the true Passion of Love bathe every pore of your body, and from that place in me where I can feel deep enjoyment, I am sending you a big embrace, full of tenderness and gratitude ... I LOVE YOU WITH ALL MY BEING.

I, Emma, AM HEALTHY, HAPPY AND I LOVE YOU DEEPLY"

The next day, we all received the following message:

"Today, April 7, 2007 at 11 o'clock AM, Emma's soul has left her body, moving on to another level of even more LOVE. The parting was painless and relatively easy. We are grateful for that,

Her daughters. Eugenia and Ella"

I was not surprised. I did not expect Emma to recover. I was privileged enough to be included in the list of people to whom she wished a little portion of her ashes be entrusted. I did a ritual during which I dispersed her ashes by the sea. Emma had once told me that as a little girl her dream was to become a psychiatrist in Canada. So it felt as if symbolically I was somehow honouring one of her deep wishes.

If I have shared with you Emma's journey, it is because I have truly seen grace at work in the way in which she both struggled with and surrendered to the deeper teachings of her failing body. I am forever grateful to Emma for having taught me that the wisdom of the body that fails us may help us heal our whole being at yet a deeper level: it may help us heal our soul.

References

Bowlby, John (1969), trad. fr. 1978, Attachement et perte, T. 1: L'attachement, Paris, PUF

Clauer, Jörg (2007) Embodied Comprehension. Treatment of Psychosomatic Disorders in Bioenergetic Analysis in The Clinical Journal of the International Institute for Bioenergetic Analysis, Vol. 17, edition psychosozial, pp. 105–133

Cozolino, Louis (2006) The Neuroscience of Human Relationships. Attachment and the Developing Social Brain. W. W. Norton. New York

Crombez, Jean-Charles (1994) La guérison en écho. Publications MNH. Montréal

Cyrulnik, Boris (2008) De chair et d'âme. Odile Jacob, Paris

Frankl, Viktor E. (2006) Découvrir un sens à sa vie. Éditions de l'Homme, Montréal. (English edition, Man's Search of Meaning. 1997, Beacon. Boston)

Janssen, Thierry (2008) La maladie a-t-elle un sens? Fayard. Paris.

Kabat-Zinn, Jon (1990) Full Catastrophe Living. Using the Wisdom of Your Body and Mind to Face Stress, Pain and Illness. Delta Trade Paperbacks. New York.

Keleman, Stanley (1985) Emotional Anatomy. Center Press. Berkeley, Calif.

King, Joan C. (2004) Cellular Wisdom. Decoding the Body's Secret Language. Celestial Arts. Berkeley.

Lowen, Alexander (1995) Joy. Penguin. N. Y.

Lowen, Alexander (1988) Love, Sex and Your Heart. MacMillan Publishing. N. Y.

Lowen, Alexander (1980) Stress and Illness. A Bioenergetic View in The Voice of the Body. Collection of various monographs published in 2005 by Bioenergetics Press, Florida.

Lowen, Alexander (1977) The Way to Vibrant Health. A Manual of Bioenergetic Exercises. Harper Colophon. Harper and Row. N. Y.

Lowen, Alexander (1975) Bioenergetics. Penguin. N. Y.

Ogden, Pat; Minton, Kekuni and Pain, Clare (2006) Trauma and the Body. A Sensorimotor Approach to Psychotherapy. W. W. Norton. N. Y.

Resneck-Sannes, Helen (2007) The Embodied Mind in The Clinical Journal of the International Institute for Bioenergetic Analysis, Vol. 17, Edition Psychosozial, pp. 39–56

Resneck-Sannes, Helen (2002) Psychobiology of Affects. Implications for a Somatic Psychotherapy in The Clinical Journal of the International Institute for Bioenergetic Analysis, Vol. 13, Number 1. Winter edition, pp. 111–122

Rossi, Ernest L. (1996) The Symptom Path to Enlightenment. Palisades Gateway Publishing. California

Ryff, C. D.; Singer, B. H. & Love, G. D. (2004). Positive health: Connecting well-being with biology. Philosophical Transactions of the Royal Society of London B, 359, 1383–1394

Scaer, Robert C. (2001) The Body Bears the Burden. Trauma, Dissociation and Disease. The Haworth Medical Press. N.Y.
Schore, Allan N. (2003) Affect Regulation and the repair of the Self. W.W. Norton. N.Y.
Schore, Allan N. (1994) Affect Regulation and the Origin of the Self. The Neurobiology of Emotional Development. Lawrence Erlbaum Associates, Hillsdale, N.J.
Shane, Morton; Shane, Estelle and Gales, Mary (1997) Intimate Attachments. Towards a New Self Psychology. The Guilford Press, New York
Sternberg, Esther M. (2001) The Balance Within. The Science Connecting Health and emotions. W.H. Freeman and Co. N.Y.
Tonella, Guy (1995) Symptômes psychosomatiques et intégration corporelle in Les Lieux du Corps, No. 2. Editions Morisset, Paris

About the Author

Louise Fréchette is a clinical psychologist. She was certified as a bioenergetic analyst in 1982 has been working ever since in private practice in Montreal. Starting in 1987, she has been teaching Bioenergetic Analysis in Canada, in the United states, in France, Belgium, Spain, Argentina and New Zealand. She has also been trained in Psychosynthesis and in Ericksonian hypnosis.

4916, rue Jean-Brillant
Montréal, Qué.
Canada
H3W 1T7
louisefrechette@videotron.ca

Bioenergetic Analysis and Community Therapy

Expanding the paradigm

Mariano Pedroza

Abstracts

English

The central theme of this paper is the reflections of a Bioenergetic Therapist on his experience of working with vulnerable communities. Although this paper refers to work with many different groups, "Vulnerable Communities" is equivalent to, "precarious human settlements", an expression more often used by international organizations (especially the UN) to refer to "favelas". The work is demonstrated by making use of two methods: Bioenergetic Analysis and Community Therapy. The search of an integration of these models suggests a possible paradigm expansion.

Key words: Bioenergetic Analysis; Community Therapy; Culture; Social webs; Grounding; Autonomy.

Bioenergetische Analyse und gemeindeorientierte Sozialarbeit: Eine Erweiterung des Paradigmas (German)

Dieser Beitrag handelt von den Reflexionen eines Bioenergetischen Analytikers über seine Arbeitserfahrungen mit "verletzlichen Gemeinschaften". Obwohl sich der Aufsatz auf die Arbeit mit vielen verschiedenen Gruppen bezieht, kann "verletzliche Gemeinschaften" mit "Elendsvierteln" gleichgesetzt werden; dies ist ein Begriff, der in Bezug auf die brasilianischen "Favelas" bei internationalen Organisationen (v. a. den UN) gebräuchlicher ist. Die Arbeit wird mit Hilfe der Anwendung von zwei Methoden vorgestellt: Bioenergetische Analyse und gemeindeorientierte Sozialarbeit. Der Versuch, diese beiden Ansätze zu integrieren, legt eine mögliche Erweiterung unseres Paradigmas nahe.

Schlüsselbegriffe: Bioenergetische Analyse; gemeindeorientierte Sozialarbeit; Kultur; Soziale Netzwerke; Erden; Autonomie

Analyse Bioénergétique et Thérapie de Communauté: En développant le paradigme (French)

Le thème central de cet article est celui des réflexions d'un thérapeute bioénergéticien sur son expérience de travail avec les communautés vulnérables. Bien que cet article se réfère au travail avec beaucoup de groupes différents, le terme les "communautés vulnérables" est équivalent à "groupes humains fragiles" une expression plus souvent utilisée par les organisations internationales (en particulier l'ONU) pour parler des "favelas". La démonstration du travail se fait à travers l'utilisation de deux méthodes: l'Analyse Bioénergétique et la thérapie communautaire. La recherche de l'intégration de ces modèles suggère un développement possible de ce paradigme.

Mots-clé: Analyse Bioénergétique; Thérapie Communautaire; Culture; Réseaux sociaux; Enracinement; Autonomie.

Análisis Bioenergético y Terapia Comunitaria: Expandiendo el paradigma (Spanish)

El tema central de este articulo son las reflexiones de un Terapeuta Bioenergético acerca de su experiencia de trabajo con comunidades vulnerables. Aunque este artículo se refiere al trabajo con muchos grupos diferentes, "Comunidades Vulnerables" es equivalente a "agrupamientos humanos precarios", una expresión utilizada a menudo por las organizaciones internacionales (especialmente las NU) para referirse a las "favelas". El trabajo se muestra utilizando dos métodos: Análisis Bioenergético y Terapia Comunitaria. La búsqueda de una integración de estos modelos apunta a una posible expansión del paradigma.

Palabras clave: Análisis Bioenergético, Terapia Comunitaria, Cultura, Redes socoales, Enraizamiento, Autonomía.

L'analisi bioenergetica e la terapia di comunità: Espandere il paradigma (Italian)

Il tema centrale di questo scritto è la riflessione di un analista bioenergetico sulla sua esperienza di lavoro con comunità vulnerabili. Per quanto qui ci si riferisca al lavoro con molti differenti gruppi, "comunità vulnerabili" è l'equivalente di "insediamenti umani precari", un'espressione spesso usata dalle organizzazioni internazionali (in particolare l'ONU) per intendere le "favelas". Il lavoro viene presentato attraverso l'utilizzo di due approcci: l'analisi bioenergetica e la psicologia di comunità. La ricerca di un'integrazione tra questi modelli suggerisce una possibile espansione del paradigma.

Parole chiave: analisi bioenergetica, terapia di comunità, cultura, reti sociali, autonomia.

Análise Bioenergética e Terapia Comunitária: Expandindo o paradigma (Portuguese)

O tema central deste artigo é as reflexões de um Terapeuta Analista Bioenergético sobre sua experiência no trabalho com comunidades vulneráveis. Apesar deste artigo se basear no trabalho com muitos grupos diferentes, refere-se ao trabalho com "Comunidades Vulneráveis" ou "assentamentos humanos precários", expressão mais freqüentemente utilizada por Organismos Internacionais (e em especial pela ONU) quando se referirem às "favelas". O trabalho é demonstrado através do uso de dois métodos: Análise Bioenergética e Terapia Comunitária. A busca pela integração desses métodos sugere uma possível expansão paradigmática.

Palavras chave: Análise Bioenergética; Terapia Comunitária; Cultura; Redes sociais; Grounding; Autonomia.

Introduction

According to the United Nations Organization, since 2008, for the first time in history, the world's urban population has exceeded its rural population. Due to the serious economic, political, social and ecological problems affecting the globalized world today, many people are forced to leave their homeland in search for opportunities for a better life in the outskirts of large cities.

The accelerated growth of suburbs and *favelas*[1] – that are turned into rather precarious housing areas for an endless number of families arriving from several different parts of the country – can be witnessed in the surroundings of all metropolises. Unemployment, inappropriate infrastructure and often degrading living conditions have weakened the families and have been the cause of feelings of powerlessness and low self-esteem, thus perpetuating the misery cycle.

---

1 *Favela*: slum, in Brazilian Portuguese.

As a resident of a large city and a therapist, I often felt insecure and powerless. My own clinical practice was very rewarding, but seemed limited and insufficient when I had to face the reality surrounding my own city. A question kept echoing in my mind: "How can I get closer, instead of feeling more and more threatened? How can I act inside these communities?" These questions were the consequence of an inner restlessness, of a need for feeling more complete and fulfilled and more deeply inserted in the social context around me.

That longing led me, in 1998, to accept the challenge of working with a group of people in communities of *"sem-terra"*[2] in Maranhão. That first attempt was rather difficult and frustrating, but taught me very precious lessons, which in 2001 allowed me to discover Community Therapy (CT) and to acquire the additional knowledge that finally provided for my insertion and action in *favelas* and vulnerable communities in general.

During the past nine years I accumulated considerable experience acting as a community therapist in different contexts. I was a founding member of MISMEC-DF (Integrated Movement for Mental and Community Health) and of a community therapy training center in Brasília, where I have been working as a trainer. I have also been leading and training facilitators for many development groups for community therapists, called "Caring for the Care-taker".

In all these contexts I have always been able to feel the influence of Bioenergetic Analysis in my way of working and to confirm the precious contribution this knowledge offers to the practice with diverse social groups. I never gave up seeing individual clients in my office, as well as Bioenergetics and Core Energetics groups, contexts in which I sometimes also feel the valuable influence of CT in my way of conducting groups and sessions.

The objective of the present paper is to present the new paradigm approach of Integrative Systemic Community Therapy for working with communities and, thus, contribute to the application of Bioenergetic Analysis in social environments. I will start by telling the story of a frustrating

---

2 *Sem-terra*: landless, idem.

experience I had with a group of rural workers and discussing the need
– and some implications – for a paradigmatic expansion in the community
work. After a summarized description of the theoretical pillars that support
the approach developed by Barreto (2005), the creator of the Community
Therapy method, I will highlight some aspects that distinguish CT as a
feasible therapy for wider systems. In closing, I will identify some relationships between Bioenergetic Analysis and Community Therapy.

1   – Report of an experience
A Fish out of Water

A frustrating Bioenergetic Analysis experience
in a low income rural group

I now intend to report a rather challenging experience with two very different groups of people that has taught me very tough lessons I shall never
forget. I believe this report will illustrate and be useful for other therapists
willing to work in similar contexts in the future.

In 1998, my wife and I were invited to join a land reform project in the state
of Maranhão. Our task was to promote the integration of the technical team –
made up by a group of graduate professionals – and a group of representatives
of landless families, coming from several parts of the state – rural people, most
of them illiterate or with a very low educational level. We were first introduced
to the group of technical advisors, whose task was to help families assimilate
new technologies, organize themselves into cooperatives and make their land
commercially productive. The group was made up of agronomic engineers,
biologists, social workers, teachers and other professionals.

We met on a daily basis for two hours, during five days. During this period we were able to carry out several group integration activities, including
revitalization exercises using bioenergetics techniques and concepts that
were easily assimilated and applied. Resistance arose when the exercises

challenged certain limits in the participants' "comfort zones", as expected, which was integrated as an additional aspect in the process towards a deeper self-perception, a common challenge in the work with Bioenergetic Analysis. On the last day, the group made an excellent evaluation and there was consensus that the process had been very useful and efficient with regard to its goal of integrating the work team.

Three months later, a three-day meeting was held with the leaders of landless families. Once again, our task was to help people to grow closer to each other in order to achieve greater unity in the group. This time we were asked to work with the group of rural leaders. At the end of each work day we had one hour for meeting and working on promoting greater integration.

Since the very beginning, when I introduced myself to the group and started talking about the nature of the work we would be carrying out together, I noticed the awkward expressions and the silence hanging over the room, indicating that my words did not seem to mean what I was trying to say. I immediately felt displaced, as if I were speaking a foreign language. I tried to communicate using the most simple words I could, but it was not a matter of the complexity of the Portuguese language I was using, but rather the lack of familiarity with the proposal itself and the way it was being presented.

The reality we faced during those days quickly brought to light the limitations of our concepts and techniques for dealing with that context. Due to our naivete regarding the possibilities of application of Bioenergetic Analysis resources – at least in the way we had learned – and our absolute lack of experience with that type of audience, had caused us to accept a mission for which – at the time – we were not qualified. The group did its best and tried, as much as possible, to follow our instructions. We, on the other hand, tried to feel and perceive the reactions of people, trying to position ourselves and to somehow adapt the exercises and group dynamics we were proposing. Thanks to the goodwill available on both sides, our work was not a complete failure, but we left the first meeting with the clear feeling that we were facing a challenge greater than we could handle.

We spent long hours in anguish, trying to be creative and to conceive ways of adapting our work to that peculiar setting. I will not describe the dynamics we used in detail, but today, after a few years of experience working in social exclusion contexts, I can say that the concepts and techniques of Bioenergetic Analysis are valid and can be properly applied, as long as there is a "cultural translation" of such concepts. That requires an understanding of the culture as a code of communication and symbolic references and a certain degree of experience by the therapist as a "translator of codes". It also requires humbleness and an open mind for learning with the community, on equal terms.

2   – The need for paradigm expansion

> "Without the individual, there is no community and without community, even the free and self-secured individual cannot in the long run prosper." (Jung)

2.1   From unitary to COMM-unitary

Two basic pillars of Reich's theory and of Bioenergetics are: the concept of *functional unit*, which allows us to perceive the biological and psychological dimensions as aspects of the same energetic phenomenon, and the concept of *character*, which provides the basis for our understanding of the formation and functioning of personality as a synthesis of the shock between the natural biological impulses and the process of adaptation to culture and its rules for social living. As Lowen (1985:11) said: "Bioenergetics is a way of understanding personality through the body and its energetic processes (…) the amount of energy a person has and how she uses it determines how she responds to life's situations."

Our work is built on this way of perceiving the individual, based on his energetic functioning. In our clinical practice we use the knowledge we have of the body's energetic processes and our understanding of how such processes echo in our relationships and in life as a whole. That is a very useful perspective: when we include the body's involuntary processes in our work, we are able to access, to understand and to intervene in the unconscious functioning of our client at a very deep level.

Nevertheless, since this approach is very much centered on the *individual*, it is insufficient for facing the complexity of the contexts provided by vulnerable *communities*. Issues such as unemployment, social violence, migration, ethnical, cultural and religious differences and others that characterize today's communities lead to a loss of grounding by individuals and families. Such issues are systemic in nature and cannot be addressed in an isolated manner – they call for collective and self-sustainable solutions.

We need a perspective or paradigm that may provide a more encompassing understanding of such multidimensional issues and that may lead to an intervention model capable of responding to such challenges. Such a new perspective implies in, without losing sight of the *individual* and his particular web of relationships, perceiving the *community* as the "client" to be served. Only such essential change in our approach – from the individual to the collective, from the "unitary" to the "communitary" – will enable us to conceive ways of responding to the challenges faced by low income populations.

That was the change in approach that I lacked when, in my naivety, I did my best to work with that group of people coming from communities of landless workers in Maranhão. I recognized that my own resources were not sufficient for dealing with that challenge, but at that time I could not assess precisely what was missing. Three years later, when I met professor Adalberto Barreto and the trans-disciplinary model of CT, I finally was able to integrate the "failure" I had experienced and acquire the understanding and the technical tools required for acting as a therapist in contexts of social exclusion.

2.2   A trans-disciplinary perspective

A few implications of this change from the unitary to the communitary approach must be considered. When we acknowledge the community as "the client", we must go way beyond a purely bio-psychological concept of human issues and include social and cultural dimensions. Therefore, we must open ourselves to the contributions provided by other fields of knowledge.

It is worth remembering that Reich, in his search to expand the clinical work in order to allow for greater social coverage, started a greater personal involvement with the social movements of his time. He had to reach beyond the psychoanalytical theory and include sociological, pedagogical and anthropological theories. Through his involvement with "proletarian" communities, Reich also acknowledged the need for a trans-disciplinary paradigm.

This paper does not intend to discuss the theory of Community Therapy (CT) in depth. Nevertheless, in order to allow readers to better understand the topic, I will briefly introduce its theoretical pillars: systemic thinking, cultural anthropology, the theory of communication, resilience and the pedagogy of Paulo Freire.

Systemic thinking says that "crises and problems only can be understood and solved if we perceive them as integrating parts of a complex network filled with ramifications that provide for connections and relationships among people within a whole that involves the biological dimension (the body), the psychological dimension (mind and emotions) and society. Everything is connected, every part depends on the other parts. We are a whole, in which each part influences and interferes with the other parts" (BARRETO 2005: XX).

Cultural anthropology says that, "culture can be understood as a reference to be used by each group member for assessing and distinguishing values, for thinking and making choices in life. Culture is a code, an essential element of reference for our personal and our group identity" (BARRETO 2005: XXII).

Theory of communication says that communication between people is the bond that holds individuals, families and societies together. Every behavior – either verbal or not, individual or by a group – is a communication. Ambiguous communication is harmful to relationships. Therefore, it is extremely important that we search for clarity and sincerity in communication, since that can be a real tool for transformation and growth.

The concept of resilience allows us to understand that the process of facing difficulties and overcoming adversities leads to the acquisition of experience-based knowledge. Namely, where there is suffering, there's a possibility for human growth. Focusing only on the shortcomings, on what "does not work", may lead to a feeling of powerlessness and reduced self-esteem. According to Barreto (2005: XXV), "The essential goal of Community Therapy is identifying and awakening the strengths and skills of individuals, families and communities so that they may, through these resources, find their own solutions and overcome the difficulties imposed by their environment and by society."

Paulo Freire's pedagogy shows us that willingness for dialog with people, sharing and exchanging experiences is a pre-condition for working with communities. To teach is an exercise of dialog, exchange, reciprocity. Freire (1983: 95) says:

> "Self-sufficiency does not go with dialog. Men that lack humbleness or have lost it cannot get close to the people. They cannot be their companions in pronouncing the world. Someone incapable of feeling and knowing himself as much a man as the other still has a long way to go before he reaches the place where he can meet them. At this meeting place, no one is absolutely ignorant or absolutely wise: there are only men seeking to know more in communion."

3   – A coherent structure in unforeseeable contexts

CT is characterized by being a very simple model, applicable to an endless number of contexts and physical conditions, and applicable to different populations and age groups. When the context is marked by the unexpected, by uncertainty and frequent and disconcerting emergency situations, establishing an inflexible service model is impossible. The reality of such contexts always requires "presence of mind", flexibility and creativity for dealing with the unexpected. On the other hand, if we do not have a very clear axis for conducting our work, we are at risk of losing the course during the session, opening the way for confusing or even chaotic situations.

Therefore, a CT session is structured into clearly defined stages – welcome/theme selection/contextualization/problematization/aggregation rituals/evaluation – establishing a "backbone" for a coherent conduction, with a beginning, a middle and an end. Simple and clear rules – remaining silent in order to listen to the one who is talking/talking about one's own experience in the first person/no advice giving or lecturing or preaching/singing known songs, telling jokes, stories or quoting sayings associated to the topic being discussed – determine that each person shall talk only about his or her own experience and avoids that others may position themselves as if they knew best with regard to the other person's life, judging, counseling or lecturing.

Thus, the CT structure allows to simultaneously serve a large number of people in a multiplicity of contexts. In my practice as therapist, I had the opportunity to participate in sessions with groups of 6 up to 200 people in places as different as health care stations in the periphery; public hospital corridors; doing "itinerant therapy" in the homes of community residents; in the shed used for community gathering; the public square; the patio of a prison and others.

I believe it is worth mentioning that CT circles usually are open to the public and anyone can show up without prior notice and without committing him or herself to continue a process. There also are no restrictions whatsoever with regard to age, sex, ethnicity, religion or relationship among participants. Such openness allows for multiple group configurations, which come up spontaneously, without excluding anyone. It also allows people that are interested in just getting familiar with the proposal to participate without any obligation to speak. The combination of a simultaneously well-structured and flexible session allows the therapist to deal with the unforeseeable nature of the context, without losing the "thread", and offers the community the freedom to self-regulate its own process. As highlighted by Grandesso (2004), in her article *"Terapia Comunitária – Um contexto de fortalecimento de indivíduos, famílias e redes"*:

> "Additionally, Community Therapy does not depend on the same people giving continuity to the therapeutic process, session after session, thus expanding its reach and feasibility even further. It is a special therapy model in which each session has the character of a therapeutic act[3], with a beginning, a middle and an end for those people attending the session on that day. On the other hand, if we consider that a major part of the group may attend the therapy sessions on a more or less regular basis, we also can consider that, for the community, the Community Therapy ends up becoming a therapeutic process carried out along time."

3.1 A structure with an "orgastic curve"

The structure of a CT session leads to Reich's concept of an *orgastic curve*. The welcome phase starts the group integration process, establishing the "rules of the game" and allowing people to relax by using playful body dynamics. The selection of a theme raises the tension and provides for space for people to expose the issues they wish to address, identifying the focus of the group energy and choosing the topic to be worked with in depth. Next, during the contextualization stage, one person reports his or her story and the group asks questions, leading to a progressive increase of the tension and of the session's emotional load. When the climax is reached, when the people have identified themselves to a high degree and have gotten involved in the topic, the "motto" – a key question that will allow for the group's reflection during the therapy – is put on the table, starting the

---

3 This expression was a contribution of psychologist and therapist Sônia Fonseca, a trainee at the NUFAC-PUC-SP-2003 Community Therapy course, based on her experience as a psychodramatist.

problematization stage. The accumulated energy can then be discharged. People that identified themselves with the topic may now let out, sharing their own experiences associated to the topic. After a satisfactory discharge, the group stands up and forms a very tight circle for the aggregation ritual stage. The therapist thanks the group for its trust and gives feedback to the participants that exposed themselves, giving a positive connotation to the stories told. People feel touched, relieved and can relax in the group's solidarity embrace. After the good-byes, the team of therapists internally reflects about each stage of the session during the evaluation stage.

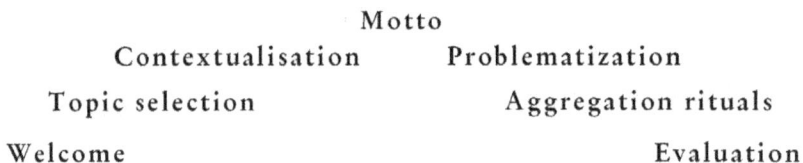

Motto	
Contextualisation	Problematization
Topic selection	Aggregation rituals
Welcome	Evaluation

4   – In search of an integration

Along the years, through my work as a Bioenergetic Analyst and Community Therapist, a few aspects of both approaches – Bioenergetic Analysis and Community Therapy – have been the object of much deeper thinking. I will briefly analyze these aspects that provide the basis for my practice and that illustrate the way how the two approaches integrate and complement each other.

4.1   The body, a transcultural basis

"The body is the beach of the ocean of being." – Sufi (anonymous)

An important aspect regarding the contribution that body psychotherapies can give to group work in several different cultures must be highlighted: working with a biological basis is a universal fact. Ekman (1999) defines "basic emotions" as the emotions that can be identified in the corporal expression and, most of all, by the facial expression of people, transculturaly. Every human being, irrespective of race or culture, has a body, breathes, moves and gets emotional. As we all know, at the basis of our bio-psychological functioning, there are deep energetic processes – charge/discharge, flow/blocking, tension/relaxation, etc. – governed to a great extent by physiological mechanisms associated to the primitive, instinctive parts of our brain and nervous system that are not under our conscious control. That becomes very obvious when we face traumatic situations that threaten our lives and that activate our survival instinct. According to Levine (1999, 19): "Even though our intellect often supersedes our natural instincts, it does not command the traumatic reaction. We are more similar to our four-legged friends than we like to think."

The fact that Bioenergetic Analysis offers a deep understanding of the expressive resources, of the involuntary movements – in short, of the energetic functioning of the organism – allows for the development of psychocorporal work that is extremely beneficial for people in any culture. David Berceli, for example, developed a simple sequence of exercises, capable of producing waves of involuntary movements (neurogenic tremors) that help dissolve chronic tensions from specific muscle groups associated to the freezing state produced by traumatic experiences. His exercises have helped many traumatized people and have been successfully applied to populations from very different cultures.

I am convinced today that other sequences can be developed with different purposes and that, as Bioenergetics therapists, we are in a position to contribute enormously to the work carried out with communities in several different cultural contexts.

4.2   Culture: Poison and Remedy

Reich and Freud held meetings for debating the relationship between civilization and neurosis, particularly with regard to whether sexual repression and the frustration of the instinct were necessary for our cultural formation (Boadella, 1985). Such discussions were especially relevant with regard to the search for a broader social intervention. I think that this debate remains valid and up to date, since ecology or man's relationship with nature is an issue that remains far from a solution, calling for effective answers on which our very survival as a species may depend upon.

The ecological imbalance produced by man's action on the planet reflects the imbalanced relationship that man has with his own nature. Culture imposes a conditioning that usually gets into conflict with the vital impulses of the child, forcing it to develop an "adaptation strategy" – the formation of character. Such strategy implies – at least partially – in the building up of an armor by the body and, to a greater or lesser extent, in a personality splitting that – at best – leads to neurosis. In this sense, culture can be viewed as a "poison" that castrates and distorts the nature of the child.

On the other hand, culture is an important organizing reference for social relationships and is the cornerstone of the constitution of identity, a heritage that links us to the knowledge of our ancestors. The loss of such reference would imply – at least partially – in losing ourselves. This is recognized today by the United Nations Organization. According to the Universal Declaration on Cultural Diversity (article 1):

> "Culture takes diverse forms across time and space. This diversity is embodied in the uniqueness and plurality of the identities of the groups and societies making up humankind. As a source of exchange, innovation and creativity, cultural diversity is as necessary for humankind as biodiversity is for nature. In this sense, it is the common heritage of humanity and should be recognized and affirmed for the benefit of present and future generations."

Especially in working with communities, there is no doubt that the rescue of values, references and cultural expressions is a "remedy" that helps people that have been upset by the loss of their origins to reestablish a feeling of belonging and self-esteem.

4.3   Translating "Cultural Codes"

As mentioned before, with its knowledge on the energetic functioning of the body and its technical possibilities, Bioenergetic Analysis can contribute with practical and potentially universal tools to the work with diverse populations. On the other hand, it also became clear that for humans, culture may be just as determining as biology and must be taken into account. As reported in my first experience with rural workers in Maranhão, I experienced serious difficulties in applying bioenergetics concepts and techniques to that group. The concepts and techniques were not inadequate for those people. What produced an "awkward feeling" was my inability to understand and use the appropriate "cultural codes". Culture is a multidimensional communication code that, in addition to the verbal code – the language – includes gesture codes, musical codes, scent codes, etc.

When I joined the first training group for community therapists in Brasília, in 2001, the modules – a happy surprise – already included breathing exercises, movement and emotional expression. Since then, I have learned very, very much from watching how Barreto culturally adapts the dynamics, translating concepts and work objectives into images, sayings, tales and metaphors taken from popular knowledge. In his words: "culture is a code and the therapist must be a translator of codes."

A very useful element for adapting our techniques to the community context is the use of rituals. By conducting CT groups, I learned to properly integrate technical tools from Bioenergetic Analysis that were very useful in helping to dissolve blockages imposed by the armor by using "rituals". As an illustration, I will report a situation in which an elderly woman, whom I will call *Dona Tereza*, tried to speak out and lost her voice. I told her she didn't have to hurry, asked her to breathe and to start talking when she was ready. In her second attempt, she started a sentence and then got stuck again. I noticed the strong throat block that kept her from expressing herself. After her third attempt, she wanted to give up speaking. I then asked her and the whole group to stand up. Told them we would do an exercise for getting rid of the blockages and burdens that suffocated and strangled us:

"Let's remember all the times we had to *swallow a frog*[4], swallow our tears, to lower our heads and shut up … "

With the feet firmly on the floor, breathing in deeply, we raised our hands up high as if we were grasping a heavy burden and, screaming out loud, we threw this imaginary weight on the floor in the middle of the circle. The group, strongly identified with Dona Tereza, performed the movement and yelled out vehemently, and Dona Tereza, no longer feeling the focus of all attention, gave in to the exercise. After a few collective screams, we set down again and Dona Tereza spoke out.

Had I tried to unblock Dona Tereza's throat individually in front of the group, I probably would have failed and she would have felt exposed. By "ritualizing" the exercise and transforming it into a collective dynamic, Dona Tereza felt protected and supported, instead of feeling exposed, and the group as a whole benefitted from the expressive body work.

4.4   Bioenergetics in a "favela"

In the beginning of this paper I described my first attempt to use bioenergetics with a group of landless rural workers and the difficulties I had in dealing with the challenges I was faced with. Since then, the years of practice with CT have given me the means to insert myself in "favelas", bond and build trust, creating conditions to also introduce Bioenergetics in a manner that makes it accessible to a broader range of people. There are basically three different contexts in which I use Bioenergetics associated with community work:

1)   In the training groups for Community Therapists – in this case, body oriented psychotherapeutic work is an integral part of the training. Although there are usually some participants who live in "favelas",

---

4 "To swallow a frog" is an idiomatic expression that means the person in a given situation had to swallow her words and her feelings.

the group is usually mixed with highly educated people. This setting is therefore closer to other training groups;

2) During CT sessions – either as a warm up before the session (similar to an exercise class) or, as in the example with Dona Tereza, as an element of the session to help someone or the group overcome a specific difficulty;

3) In groups organized in the community for "Stress Management and rescue of Self-Esteem" – We usually organize such groups when we already have built a relationship of trust with a good number of community members. In this setting, intense bioenergetic work can be appropriately used with populations at risk[5].

In order to give the reader a clearer idea of how Bioenergetics knowledge and techniques can be successfully applied in contexts of vulnerable communities, I will now present a session that I was invited to lead in Pirambu, one of the biggest "favelas" of Fortaleza, in Ceará, birthplace of Community Therapy. I will also stress some specific elements in the way the work was conducted that made the difference in terms of how the group grasped the concepts and surrendered to the experience.

It is important to mention that because the project has existed in that community for many years, a bond of trust already existed. The group was large, about 80 participants of different ages and although many people were there for the first time, there were also many participants who were already familiar with this kind of work. This allowed me to risk going into an intense work.

Introduction: To begin with, I explained that the exercises we were going to do were "good for our health", that they were meant to help us "get rid of tensions and stress that accumulate in our bodies and make us suffer, provoking insomnia, depression, illnesses etc". I also said that the techniques we

---

5 "populations at risk" is commonly used by the United Nations to refer to populations living in very precarious conditions where there is lack of access to basic infrastructure and services such as education, health care etc.

would use were safe, they have helped thousands of people, of all different kinds of background and religions, in many different cities and countries. *It is important to notice that this kind of language can be instantaneously understood because it refers directly to the reality of the great majority of the group, it speaks directly to their experience and suffering.*

Building a safe environment: Next, I used a process that I learned from Barreto to create a safe setting. In pairs, in a circle, one person (A) stands with the eyes closed and knees slightly bent. The second person (B) – the "guardian angel" or "care-taker" – stands behind (A) placing the hands on his/her shoulders. With soft music on the background, the "guardian angels", while doing a "massage" on the shoulders of the "protected ones", were asked to repeat about three times, in a low voice, the following sentences: "Who are you?"; "What is your pain or your suffering?"; "What have you been learning from it?"; "What have you been doing for yourself?"; "Know that you are not alone, you can count on me!" While each sentence is slowly and repeatedly pronounced by the "guardian angel" (A), (B) remains silent, only feeling, breathing and listening to the inner resonance, inner answers. For some people this experience already touched deep emotions, the room was filled with a calm, dense atmosphere. Some people, as they later shared, had never had a reference of a safe, protecting presence in their lives. After changing roles, we were ready to begin the body work.

Notice that the sentences used suggest that we can grow from our pain/ suffering (resilience). There is also an emphasis on bringing about the support that exists in the group, and to create a sense of belonging as opposed to being alone. The "collective or social dimension" is often underlined in the work.

Grounding and building charge: More dispersed in the room, I told the group to close their eyes as I told them a short tale: "One day a man was sad, disappointed with life, depressed, thinking of ending his life. As he walked towards a cliff, he met a big tree, so filled with life, with such bright colors and sweet fruits. He was so surprised with that tree that he stopped in front of it in admiration. In silence, he asked the tree – Please, tell me your secret, if life is so sad, painful, so rotten, how can you be so colorful and give such sweet fruits? In its silence, the tree answered – In my deepest roots, I have learned to take all the garbage, all rotten things, and transform them into nutrients, this is what helps me to grow strong and colorful and give good fruits." I explained that, like the tree, we need deep roots in order to grow strong and give "good fruits". The body work that followed was all the time associated to the image of the tree. So, during the day, the trees will look for the sunlight, spread their branches to "find a place under the sun" (hands up reaching towards the sky, movements with the arms etc – *limits/individuality*) and at the same time they need to cooperate in order to create a forest (*inter-dependence, collectivity*). At night the trees move all their sap (juice of the plant) to their roots (relax the arms, neck, bend forward, move toes, feet etc). Using such images, we alternated between stress positions, stretches, the "wind blowing" would help to open the breathing etc.

Expression and discharge: I said that in the forest, there is a tribe of warriors preparing to fight. Many enemies – depression; fear; despair; stress; worries; insomnia etc – were trying to destroy this tribe. To stimulate sound and go into more expressive work, I used a very simple game that children play very spontaneously in many different cultures: I asked everyone to simply imitate me, my gestures and my sounds. I then began, in a "playful" way, to move and open my voice. As the group responded, I used rhythm as a way to establish a common pace and strengthen the "collective field" or "container". Many variations were used, moving sideways in the circle stamping our feet and voicing different vowels, inverting the direction, placing two fingers below eyes and looking into the eyes of other group members etc. Sometimes we would go into more aggressive expressions, somewhat similar to warriors in a ritual preparing for war. As the group responded, we went more and more into strong expressive gestures and sounds, including key words like "no" or "get away" etc.

At a certain peak moment, we moved into a tight circle with our arms around each other forming a firm group embrace. I told the group that nowadays we see a lot of violence and crime, the level of fear is very high, and when we are afraid our bodies shrink and get tight and tense. I said we would get the fear out of our bodies. Remaining in the tight embrace, with our knees bent, and lifting our heels off the ground, many people started vibrating. Then, with the feet firm on the ground, eyes wide open, I said that we would let the fear out using a high pitched scream. The group responded strongly, and a few people went hysterical, screaming and stamping their feet – *had they not been held tight in the group embrace they would have been running the risk to hurt themselves.* At this point we started making a strong low pitched sound and started stamping our heels on the floor to bring the energy down. We then moved gradually into softer sounds and movements that helped to ground the group (stamping our feet rhythmically, bending and stretching the knees etc). When it felt safer, we let go of the tight embrace but kept in contact holding our arms, later moving on to holding hands until we could finally let go of our hands and be silent for a moment. Three "old timers" started spreading mattresses around the room.

One important element that, in my perspective, makes this kind of work safe with such a big group is the permanent use of elements that strengthen the "container", the "collective field". You can notice that I didn't stop leading the group to deal with the people who were flooding. On the contrary, I focused on grounding the group as a whole. The field created by such a big group is extremely powerful. If a strong "current" is created – by the use of rhythm for example – the individuals who are momentarily flooded can be "pulled back" by the "current". In the example above, it is important to also notice that the "group embrace" created a very safe holding, making it possible to have some hysteria without risk of anyone getting hurt. Had I stopped to deal with the floodings individually, the "current" would have been fragmented and the group would have been at risk.

Integration and sharing: Everyone laid down on their backs with their eyes closed. With soft music on the background, they were asked to breathe in through the nose and breathe out through their mouth … breathing in new life … and breathing out all their worries into a balloon … then watching the balloon move up to the sky until it disappeared. Then they were asked to imagine they were laying on wet earth or clay … and to allow the earth to pull the toxins, poisons etc out of their bodies … and then to draw with their inner vision the shape of their bodies on the floor ... then they imagined a waterfall with clear water near them and they cleaned themselves in the pure water ... and dried themselves in the sun and the breeze. Then, still with their eyes closed, they were asked to reach and find the hands of the people next to them ... and feel that there are other people who are looking for a healthy, peaceful life, other people who are "walking the same path" ... to conclude, they placed one hand on the heart and the other on the belly ... "feel that you can also count on yourself".

They were then asked to sit down. I explained that after this kind of work, we always give people the opportunity to share their experience or ask questions. First of all because we learn a lot from each other´s experiences and second because some people might have felt or experienced things that they didn't understand and it is important to have the space to talk about it. As we do during a Community Therapy session, people were allowed to interrupt at any moment with songs, poems etc, related to the theme that was being shared. The sharing allowed more time for people to integrate the experience. As usual in these sharings, people expressed pieces of their experience that were either more intense, or more meaningful to them. Some people made direct connections with their life history, others needed some help, through questions, to make some connections. When deep feelings were touched again, the songs would serve as a soothing element, allowing time for the person to be with the feeling and at the same time helping the energy to flow in the group. After about thirty minutes of sharing, we stood up and gave "at least ten hugs" before leaving the room.

As I have mentioned before, the bioenergetic principles, concepts and exercises can give an important contribution for the work with populations at risk, and there are many different ways in which sessions can be structured in order to be appropriately used in such contexts. In my experience, a few simple aspects make the difference in terms of how the group assimilates the directions of the facilitator and responds to the work: 1) Introducing the work in very simple terms, making direct reference to the real issues that make people suffer in their daily lives (stress; depression; fear; insomnia etc); 2) Using a diversity of codes (verbal, images, music, movement etc.)

– some people will be resistant to the verbal code but will respond easily to rhythm and movement for example; 3) Using elements that will stress and strengthen the collective field, the group cohesion, the social dimension, the sense of belonging, of trust in the group, group support etc. When these elements are creatively included in the structure of the session, a safe setting is created and the group responds.

4.5   The "community body"

According to Lowen (1985, 11), "Bioenergetics is a form of therapy that combines work with the body and the mind to help people resolve their emotional problems and realize more of their potential for pleasure and joy in living". The body is central in Bioenergetics clinical work, as it reveals so much about who the person is. In the body we can identify the wounds, the distortions and compensations caused by the history of life. The body also reveals the vital force and the creative resources that are available to the person. Bioenergetic Analysis considers that the body has its own wisdom and a great potential for resilience, that is, a great capacity to overcome traumatic situations and, in the process of overcoming, to transform suffering into learning and growth. The work we do while helping the client to "re-connect" himself to his body, aims to create favorable conditions for the body to rescue its vitality and its own path towards recovery. In other words, we trust the body and we try to encourage its natural capacity to overcome its own limitations.

The same principles can be applied when working with a community. We can conceive a "community body". The community, as well as the individual, presents symptoms that derive from painful events that generated fear, violence, disaggregation, fragmentation. The "community body" also develops "defenses" and "blocks" that hinder the integration and the natural and creative flow of vital energy. To a certain extent, we can apply our Bioenergetics paradigm to the "community body". We can trust the living organism – the community – and search for ways of promoting clear and sincere communication, bringing people closer to each other, strengthening the ties and reducing the level of fragmentation of the "social tissue". That allows the creativity of the community itself to manifest, opening the way for resources and solutions for existing problems, both individual and collective ones.

In Bioenergetics clinical work, body reading provides information that is very precious for the therapeutic process. Among other things, it helps to diagnose the person's degree of fragmentation, as well as to identify where her strength and possibilities are. We can also "read" the "community body", but the main tool for diagnosing the degree of fragmentation and for identifying where and how energy either flows or is blocked is assessing the *quantity and quality of ties* between community members.

Therefore, it is essential for the work to lead to the strengthening of relationships between people, because individuals will find support and strength for overcoming challenges and fighting for their dreams in their "network of ties". The deeper the emotional ties, the greater the union and cohesion of the "community body", allowing it to find its own creative exits for its deadlocks.

4.6   Grounding and Community Therapy

> "In a much broader sense, grounding represents an individual's contact with the basic realities of his existence" (Lowen: 1985, 23).

The concept of Grounding is key in Bioenergetic Analysis theory and practice and may be understood as a "rooting in the earth", i. e., the person's capacity to enter into contact with herself and with the outside world. In *Grounding e Autonomia*, Weigand (2006) presents the historical evolution of the concept of Grounding, including valuable contributions from other psycho-corporal, analytical and systemic approaches that helped to expand our understanding and our interventions. The author differentiates between several types of grounding, including: postural grounding, internal grounding, grounding thru the eyes, grounding in the family, in the culture and others. Such expansion of the Grounding concept is essential for working with communities, since it offers new possible directions for promoting the strengthening of the "rooting in the earth", especially when dealing with poor populations, with limited resources. Next I will share a few considerations on the elements that, in my perspective, promote grounding during a CT session and develop the grounding of the community along time.

As mentioned earlier, the established structure and rules provide a "basis", a "ground" and – why not – a grounding for the therapist to conduct the process. But there are also other aspects of CT that promote the grounding of individuals, of the group and of the community that deserve being highlighted: the narrative process as a means for building *internal grounding*; the use of the collective energy field as a *continent*; the horizontal pulsation of energy as *relationship grounding*; grounding in the family, in the community and in the culture.

"Having a substantiated understanding corresponds to having one's *feet firmly planted on the ground*. Such ground *needs* to be both material and symbolic" (Weigand: 2006, 45). One of the ways by which such "symbolic ground" is strengthened in CT is through the practice of the narrative. Trauma studies have shown that a traumatized person tends to narrate events in a fragmented and confused manner. The narrative is jeopardized, hampering the integration of the experience. We may say that the person "lost her ground" and tends to build limited and imprisoning narratives. During the session, the group – while preparing questions in an attempt to obtain a clearer understanding of the story being told – exercises its capacity to focus, to listen and to understand. While answering the questions, the individual exercises his capacity to set his experience into words, expressing himself with clarity and, at the same time, processing the feelings that come up, since reports usually are highly loaded with emotion. Thus, by reporting a painful or an even traumatic experience, the person is helped in the reconstruction of her narrative, which equals an internal reorganization of the experience, both emotionally and cognitively and, as a consequence, a strengthening of her *internal grounding*.

Stories told by individuals during a session can be considered as the *content* and the group's collective energy field is the *continent* that receives, provides support and helps to process it. I remember how John Pierrakos, when working with someone, would sometimes turn to the group and say: "Come on! Breathe!" He always kept an eye on the individual and another on the group. He was aware of the fact that, whenever the group holds the flow of energy, working with the individual will be more difficult. In CT, the session's grounding is supported to a great extent by the cohesion of the group's energy field. Creative interventions can be used – such as jokes, poems, sayings and especially songs – and they often are offered by the group itself, transferring the focus of attention from the individual to the collective, thus helping the energy to circulate. That strengthens the *continent* (the circle), which on its turn favors working with the *content* (the emotional narratives of individuals). This resource is especially important when the emotional load is too intense or when the content of the discourse is too heavy: once the energy flows around in the circle, it can alleviate the person, adding lightness and fluidity to the process.

Another extremely important dimension of grounding during CT sessions is benefitting from the horizontal pulsation of energy. According to Weigand (2006, 47), "Horizontal pulsation corresponds to the grounding created through relationships. Such pulsation flows from the genitals, from the heart, from the solar plexus, from the throat and from the eyes. It is responsible for communicating with others and with external objects." By creating an environment that welcomes feelings, CT promotes a sincere communication between people and grounding through horizontal pulsation. The group's careful and respectful listening produces a fertile environment for resonance and mirroring that strengthen the feelings of union, supporting the process as a whole.

CT being a systemic approach, we always try to strengthen family grounding. When contextualizing the issue presented by someone, it is important to include the family system – both the nuclear and the extended family – in the vision field. Simple and direct questions regarding the family structure helps us see how the person is inserted in the context of the family system's relational dynamics. Such contextualization usually produces new awareness movements, bringing into light aspects of the narrator's history that had been there only as a backdrop. On one hand, "invoking" the family system facilitates the processing of "pending issues", such as incomplete mourning, ancient griefs, foul relational dynamics, etc. On the other hand, it helps the person to recognize and rescue existing resources from its family basis, such as figures that represent emotional, material or even symbolic support – such as a heroic ancestor, for example – strengthening the grounding in the family.

Grounding in the community is another key dimension of grounding according to the CT model. The symbol adopted by Barreto for CT is the spider web. He adopted this symbol based on a ritual of the Tremembé Indians that dance to represent lessons learned from several animals. In order to live, the spider depends on the web she builds by herself. We may conceive the web as an important form of grounding that assures survival. Community Therapy is a model for the construction of "webs of ties" in the community. In addition to promoting the construction of solidarity relationships among participants during the sessions, habits such as trying to understand instead of judging, listening carefully and respecting differences, tend to be assimilated by the more regular attendants and spontaneously disseminated through their everyday relationships within the community. In Barreto's words (2005, 53): "(…) the group that listens ends up echoing what it heard. Those who have identified themselves may, at last, talk about what used to dwell inside them in silence. Listening arouses the desire for solidarity, awakens compassion, outlining the first steps towards the construction of a solidary community."

Cultural roots are always strengthened by CT sessions. Cultural anthropology states that identity is closely associated to culture. Who "I am" includes the clothes I wear, the food I eat, the songs and dances I know, the feasts, rituals, traditions and values of my ancestors. The loss of such references jeopardizes the self-esteem of migrants and produces a feeling of inadequacy and frailty. By opening room for cultural expressions – popular songs, sayings, stories and others – CT promotes the legitimation of the cultural framework of each individual and of the community's cultural diversity. That is a very deep way of rescuing the roots, i.e., of "rooting in" or *grounding in culture*. Besides, it also teaches us to understand that differences are assets that expand the group's possibilities.

4.7 Generating Autonomy

In 1992, Lowen, (in Weigand 2006: 36) stated that, "for him the objective of bioenergetics psychotherapy was self-perception, self-expression and self-possession, that is, knowing oneself, expressing one's own truth and being our own boss".

Bioenergetic Analysis tries to deepen the person's awareness about her corporal and emotional reality and considers that being identified with the reality of one's own body is essential for the individual's health. BA also tries to rescue the expressive resources, especially the voice and the gestures, that were hampered along life, so that the person may be capable, not only of perceiving, but also of expressing what she feels in her relationships, in a true and appropriate manner. Lastly, Bioenergetics aims to encourage the autonomy of people. Working with limits, the expression of the "no", different forms of grounding and, during the process, strengthening the clients' confidence in their own feelings, their own perceptions and their own capacity to deal with life improves. Ideally speaking, we may consider that the client should be discharged from therapy when – being in contact with the truth of his feelings and aware of both, his limitations and his resources and potential – he takes responsibility for his process and takes his life into his own hands.

CT, as mentioned before, promotes the integration of the "community body", facilitating the processing of suffering and the establishment of bonds and developing *social network of solidaritys*. By reaching beyond the unitary towards the communitary, CT does not intend to solve problems, but rather to highlight the community's own capacity to search for collective solutions for its impasses. By rescuing the knowledge and the competence deriving from the resilient process of overcoming adversities and by acknowledging such knowledge within the community itself, CT looks beyond the shortages in order to highlight the competences, thus encouraging the feeling of self-confidence and self-responsibility. By leaving behind verticality in order to promote horizontal relationships, CT welcomes, acknowledges and supports those who are experiencing situations of suffering. The diversity of cultural experiences, know-how and roots that are present in groups and communities adds value and is then understood as wealth. Collective learning generates a dynamic of inclusion and empowerment in the community.

In their work with low income populations, *assistentialistic* models of intervention tend to position themselves as "saviors", trying to bring pseudo-solutions from the outside to the inside, nurturing the idea and the feeling that the community is incapable of solving its own problems. We must overcome dependence-generating models that always require the presence of an expert, the "one who owns the knowledge", that brings ready-made solutions to the population. Barreto (2005, 59) says:

> "CT is a tool that allows us to build social networks of solidarity that promote life, and to mobilize the resources and competences of individuals, families and communities. We try to bring out the therapeutic dimension of the group itself, acknowledging the cultural heritage of our Indigenous, African, Oriental and European ancestors, as well as the knowledge produced by the experience of life itself."

Another aspect that deserves to be highlighted with regard to the development of community autonomy is the training of *multipliers*. CT is not a model for indiscriminate use and requires capacity building and supervision. But it is a model that allows the capacity building of a very broad universe of people, including community leaders, even if they do not hold any degree. Communities in situation of risk are increasing at a high speed and we will never be capable of responding to such widespread and increasing demand in an efficient manner if we do not develop models that can be multiplied.

I already mentioned David Berceli's work with traumatized populations. While dealing with the reality of communities that have been devastated by disaster (civil war, earthquake, tsunami and others), he recognized that it was impossible to offer specialized treatment according to standard clinical models. He then prepared a sequence of well-structured and substantiated exercises that can be conducted by people from the community itself, without any academic training, who are selected and trained by him. Later on, he meets with these "multipliers" from time to time for supervision, clearing doubts that arise during their direct experience in applying the exercises with the groups they are conducting.

Levine (1999) also reports his experience with mothers and babies of neighboring groups that have been historically marked by wars and traumatizing confrontations. By drawing upon the children's natural openness and curiosity and on child songs from the cultures involved, he created a rather simple and bond-generating dynamics, capable of being quickly assimilated by women in their own communities. According to Levine, "The beauty of this approach is its simplicity and efficacy. An external facilitator starts the process, leading the first group. Afterwards, some participating mothers can be trained as facilitators for the other groups. (…) Once they are trained, the mothers become the ambassadors of peace in their own communities" (Levine: 1999, 198).

Developing *solidarity support networks* and training *multipliers* are two essential factors for developing the autonomy of communities. If the intervention model being used **only** can be practiced by specialists with long years of training, it will be just another "colonizing" model, generating dependence, and reinforcing the inability of people to address their own problems.

Final Remarks

"Caminante, no hay camino, se hace camino al andar." ("Walker, there is no path, the path is made by walking.") – Antonio Machado (Spanish poet)

At the beginning of this paper I reported the difficulties I faced during an attempt to apply Bioenergetic Analysis resources to a group of rural workers. Through my encounter with the Community Therapy model and the experience acquired along nine years working in peripheries and other exclusion contexts, I was able to assimilate concepts and forms of intervention that, from my point of view, can contribute to making Bioenergetic Analysis feasible as a model with a very broad social outreach.

In closing this paper I also want to encourage a growing number of therapists to find ways of acting in the context of diverse communities. The reality created by the accelerated growth of people in the peripheries of our cities, needs to be integrated into our professional practice. As we all know, acknowledging and dealing with reality is the only way to keep ourselves lucid instead of alienated, the essence of what we call *grounding*. Freud, Reich, Lowen and Pierrakos always started from practice and then developed their theories. We received such a valuable heritage! It is up to us to follow their examples, to continue expanding such knowledge, through direct experience of the reality provided by our own historic moment.

The Bioenergetic Analysis model has been contributing more and more to interventions in specific social groups. As a body-psychotherapy, it has potential for contributing in a trans-cultural way. Nevertheless, because it is centered mainly on the individual, its paradigm must be expanded in order for it to be applied in a much broader way. The Community Therapy model, with its trans-disciplinary perspective, helps us to devise new directions, both theoretically and technically, expanding our possibilities for working with wider systems.

Again, I wish to highlight the need to include the social and cultural dimensions into the conception of our interventions. As a consequence, we must always act in a way so as to promote the establishment and strengthening of bonds between people; as demonstrated, the web of emotional ties is the main vehicle for the integration of the "community body".

Both Bioenergetic Analysis and Community Therapy promote the strengthening of people's self-confidence and autonomy. I wish to reinforce that, with regard to working with communities, three elements are essential: the construction of *solidarity social networks* that create the means for individuals to find support in their own communities; the development of the resilience that opens the way for the group's own therapeutic potential;

and the design of models that may be multiplied and conducted by members of that same community. I'll conclude with the question that is often used for closing CT sessions: "What do I take with me today?" From where I stand now, I can say that working with communities has been extremely transforming for my personal and professional identity. I take with me the feeling of being more grounded in the world I live in, feeling more complete and fulfilled.

References

BARRETO, Adalberto de Paula (2005): *Terapia comunitária passo a passo*. Fortaleza, Gráfica LCR.

LOWEN, Alexander (1985): Exercícios de Bioenergética – o caminho para uma saúde vibrante. São Paulo, Ágora.

WEIGAND, Odila (2006): Grounding e autonomia – a terapia corporal bioenergética revisitada. São Paulo, Person.

BOADELLA, David (1985): *Nos caminhos de Reich*. São Paulo, Summus.

GRANDESSO, Marilene (2004): "Terapia Comunitária – um contexto de fortalecimento de indivíduos, famílias e redes". Artigo, mimeo.

BERCELI, David (1998): *Trauma Releasing Exercises*, mimeo

LEVINE, Peter (1999): *O Despertar do Tigre*. São Paulo, Summus.

EKMAN, Paul. (1999): Basic Emotions. In T. Dalgleish and T. Power (Eds.) *The Handbook of Cognition and Emotion*. Pp. 45–60. Sussex, U.K.: John Wiley & Sons, Ltd

ORGANIZAÇÃO DAS NAÇÕES UNIDAS – UNESCO (2001). Declaração Universal Pela Diversidade Cultural.

Interesting links for anyone wanting to learn more about Community Therapy:

www.abratecom.org.br

www.4varas.com.br

www.mismecdf.org

About the Author

Mariano Pedroza was born in Brasília in 1966. In 1975, due to political reasons, Mariano's family left Brazil and moved to Africa where they lived for eight years in three different countries – Ivory Coast, Angola and Senegal. At the age of seventeen, he moved to Boston – USA to study Jazz at Berklee College of Music and graduated in 1988. Since 1989, Mariano has experienced several therapeutic processes including – the Fisher Hoffman Process; Gestalt Therapy; Core Energetics, Bioenergetics and others.

Professional experience: 14 years of clinical experience seeing individuals, couples, families, groups and communities.

Certifications: Core Energetics Therapist, Local Trainer at UNIPAZ, Brasília. *(Trained by John Pierrakos whom he also translated for 10 years).*

Certified Bioenergetics Therapist – CBT

Certified Community Therapist, Supervisor and Trainer of the Associação Brasileira de Terapia Comunitária – ABRATECOM.

International Trainer in Trauma Releasing Exercises – T R E.

Mariano Pedroza
SMDB Conjunto 12 Bloco F Sala 201
Lago Sul – Brasília – DF 71680-120
Brasil
+55 61 8138 0972
+55 61 33392993
marianopedroza@gmail.com

The Impact of Gender on Subjectivity[1]

Fina Pla

Abstracts

English

This paper provides a reflection on the impact of gender in the construction of masculinity and femininity. Particular attention is paid to how gender stereotypes are created and how they affect people. The contribution of new concepts such as interrelatedness and bonding will be discussed in relation to their impact on psychotherapy. Specifically, ways that Bioenergetic Analysts can benefit from these new approaches and concepts will be provided.

Key words: Social Construct, Binary Functioning, Relational Matrix, Micromachismos, Liquid Love.

1 This paper was originally presented at the International Congress of Bioenergetic Analysis in Sevilla (Spain), May 2007.

Der Einfluss von Geschlechtsrollen auf unsere Subjektivität (German)

Dieser Beitrag beschäftigt sich mit der Bedeutung von Geschlechtsrollen für die Entwicklung von männlicher und weiblicher Identität. Dabei wird besonderes Augenmerk auf die Entstehung von Geschlechtsrollenstereotypen und deren Auswirkungen auf Menschen gelegt. Der Einfluss von neuen Konzepten wie Beziehung und Bindung auf die psychotherapeutische Arbeit wird diskutiert. Außerdem wird aufgezeigt, wie insbesondere Bioenergetische AnalytikerInnen von diesen neuen Herangehensweisen und Konzepten profitieren können.

Schlüsselbegriffe: Geschlechtsrollenidentität, männlich, weiblich, Aktivität, Beziehung.

L' Impact du Genre sur la Subjectivité (French)

Cet article apporte une réflexion sur l'impact du Genre dans la construction de la masculinité et de la féminité. Une attention particulière est portée sur la façon dont ces stéréotypes de Genre sont créés et comment ils affectent les personnes. La contribution de nouveaux concepts tels que l'inter-relation et l'attachement sera discutée en relation avec leur impact sur la psychothérapie. De façon plus spécifique, les façons dont les Analystes Bioénergéticiens peuvent bénéficier de ces nouvelles approches et nouveaux concepts seront donnés.

Mots-clés: identité de Genre, masculin, féminin, subjectivité, inter-relation.

El Impacto del Género en la Subjetividad (Spanish)

Este artículo ofrece una reflexión acerca del impacto del género en la costrucción de la masculinidad y la feminidad.Hace hincapié específicamente en como los estereotipos de género se originan y en como afectan a las personas.la contribución de nuevos conceptos tales como la interrelación y el vínculo se consideraran en relación a su impacto en la psicoterapia.específicamente, se proponen maneras en que los Análistas Bioenergéticos pueden beneficiarse con estos nuevos enfoques y conceptos.

Palabras clave: Constructo Social, Funcionamiento Binario, Matriz Relacional, Micromachismos, Amor Líquido.

L'impatto del genere sulla soggettività (Italian)

Questo scritto propone una riflessione sull'impatto del genere nella costruzione della virilità e della femminilità. Una particolare attenzione è rivolta a come gli stereotipi di genere si formano ed influenzano le persone. E' preso in considerazione il contributo dei nuovi concetti quali quello di bonding e di interconnessione per come impattano la psicoterapia. Specificamente l'autrice si sofferma sugli apporti di cui l'analisi bioenergetica può trarre vantaggio a partire da questi nuovi concetti.

Parole chiave: identità di genere, maschile, femminile, soggettività, interconnessione

O Impacto do Gênero na Construção da Subjetividade (Portuguese)

Este artigo traz uma reflexão sobre o impacto do gênero na construção da masculinidade e da feminilidade. Dá-se particular atenção à forma como os estereótipos são criados e como eles afetam as pessoas. A contribuição de novos conceitos como interrelacionamento e vinculação serão discutidos em relação ao seu impacto na psicoterapia. Especificamente, serão propostas algumas formas com que os Analistas Bioenergéticos possam se beneficiar a partir destes novos enfoques e conceitos.

Palavras Chave: Construção Social, Funcionamento Binário, Matriz Relacional, Micromachismos, Amor Líquido.

Introduction

I would like to start by sharing that my first contact with gender happened when I was twenty and attended the first feminist congress in Spain. I was deeply impacted and a whole new world opened to me. I needed to understand what it meant to be a woman in this world and what happened in the relationships between women and men. As a result of these concerns I first became a member of a feminist group, then a member of a women's therapy group and later I joined a women psychotherapists group. At the same time, I've been a member of different men and women's groups. Since then, my concern and curiosity with this issue has been alive, both in my private and in my professional life. But, what has happened with gender theory in the last decades and what have been its contributions?

The Feminist Movement opened the way and later, contributions from the different fields: psychology, anthropology, philosophy and history have been produced, which have given us tools to understand the dynamics of the patriarchal system and have provided us with new ways to understand reality. These theories reflect the situation in the present world, where ambivalence, change and uncertainness, prevail. They work with the concepts of multiplicity, individuality, instability, variability and complexity. They help us move away from rigid systems that have defined reality in very constrained and exclusive ways. For example, **Chodorow** speaks of masculinities and femininities, meaning that the process to internalize gender is individual and that there are different ways to live masculinity and femininity for each one of us.

These contributions allow us to reflect about how the person is structured within a gender system and what are the profound effects in his/her subjectivity. They explain how these unequal patterns originate and get reproduced with consequences in the psyche of both sexes. They show there is a binary functioning which is still present both in open and subtle ways, where men are associated with reason and culture, while women are related to body and feelings. This creates a division where the rational power is deposited in men and the affective power is deposited in women, with devastating consequences for the lives of all. By this I refer to all the pain and misunderstandings between men and women when they try to relate to each other and they attempt to live their masculinity and their femininity.

For a long time there was the belief that masculine and feminine traits had a biological basis and were innate, but gender studies have shown evidence that gender is a social construction. What was believed to be natural: masculine active, feminine passive, has been proved to be a social construct.

These theories also deconstruct the idea that only women suffer in a patriarchal system and give us the vision that both women and men are stuck and are prisoners of such a system, though in different ways. They help us understand the deep suffering women and men have to undergo if they do not fit into the accepted social roles.

Some examples follow from my practice: L. wants to be a mother and she has no partner at present. She is fighting with her sense of inadequacy for not having a partner and it is hard for her to give herself permission to make her desire real. M. is a gay man who has to work through his idealized fantasy of what it is to be a virile man and so overcome his inner sense of inadequacy. M. is a feminist woman who has to work with her denial. She needs to accept her dependency needs and give up her ideal of being a completely autonomous woman who doesn't need anyone. Then she can get involved in a relationship with her partner. B. has difficulty affirming her right to her parent's inheritance in a family where femininity is devalued. T. is torn between her desire to go to university and her partner's desire of living with a woman who takes care of him. **C.** Is depressed because her partner tells her that her body is not sexy enough and she has to resist his need to control her. **L.** is a middle-aged professor who has to face his newborn fatherhood and his clumsiness in relating to his baby son. Those are just some examples of how gender issues become present in a therapeutic process and how important it is that we understand and address them.

Contributions to psychotherapy

The conjunction between Gender theories, Attachment theories and Relational psychoanalysis has produced fruitful results. They open new windows in our theoretical concepts and bring forward new ideas that enrich our comprehension. **Winnicott, Benjamin, Stern, Chodorow** and others, redefine psychoanalysis with Attachment theory and introduce some interesting concepts. One important concept is the idea of interrelatedness where the idea of bonding is emphasized above the idea of drive. I quote **Benjamin:** "The life of a baby gets developed in a bonding network and his/her subjectivity is built through the relationships with the others" (Benjamin, 1988).

They stress the importance of interrelatedness in the construction of subjectivity. These authors overcome the idea of a linear development and support the notion that psychic structures get developed from a relational matrix, which starts with primary bonding.

In the classical oedipal model, father separated child from mother, but current research shows that the baby develops different attachment patterns with each parent that get developed at the same time. Differently than classical psychoanalysis, they recognize and value the role of mother as essential for the developing self. They also support the idea that there is a previous gender identity upon which the oedipal identity is built later.

These theories remark that there does not exist a natural feminine or masculine essence but it is from a complex unconscious process that libido gets oriented towards a masculine or feminine body. As a result, neither heterosexuality is natural, nor homosexuality unnatural, but both are the result of complex bio-psychosocial processes. I think these contributions broaden some ideas which have been present in bioenergetics and which have limited us.

Gender and gender identity: Money and Stoller

Money and Stoller are psychoanalysts who propose that there is a difference between the concept of sexual identity (which is the consequence of biological differences between sexes) from the concept of gender identity, (which would be the inner feeling of being a girl or a boy as something that gets structured on a social level).

Chodorow in her book, *The Reproduction of Mothering*, says:

> "Each body is created in an intrapsychic way and incorporates a relational unconscious story from birth which is the result of how one has been cared for and the unconscious messages received."(Chodorow, 1978)

Taking gender into account means understanding the impact of culture and at the same time the impact of our unconscious processes in our subjective choice of being a woman or being a man, being heterosexual or being homosexual, how we live our life and how society values or denigrates these differences.

The andocentric system we live in has produced a model of hegemonic masculinity associated with heterosexuality, which comes to mean something natural and excludes what is different as unnatural. Not very masculine men or homosexual men and women get excluded and are considered a problem. Again, we have to critically review how these gender biases are present in bioenergetics concerning masculinity and femininity, as well as concerning heterosexuality and homosexuality. We also have to reflect on the impact gender has upon women and men's bodies.

Consequences of the gender system:
The ideals of Masculinity and Femininity

The gender system is based upon a different set of ideals for men and women. Let us have a look at some of these ideals, as, even if they are in a process of change, their roots in our subjectivity are very deep.

Masculinity has been associated with being hard, an achiever, a provider and being autonomous. It implies a self-centered ego and a type of bonding that is often distrustful and with low empathy. The attributes of virility are defined by sexual potency and reproductive ability. In contrast to femininity, which is more focused on bonding, masculinity values autonomy, separation and distance. In their identifying process, men must repress their needs and their vulnerability, creating an emotional armor that provokes harmful effects in their psyche and in their way of relating.

The patriarchal system has legitimized the belief in the superiority of men for a long time. Still in many countries, to be a man is to have rights, while to be a woman means to have to fight for these rights. This unequal situation takes hold because of a lack of economic resources for women and also because of thought systems that still define reality only from a masculine perspective.

Luis Bonino, a psychologist who lives in Madrid, has created the term micromachismos to stress the subtle ways in which inequalities are reproduced in relationships. They would be imperceptible, almost invisible, control and power mechanisms that men do. They are strategies that restrict the personal power, autonomy and psychic welfare of women. They are woven like a network that grabs women and leaves them in only an availability role towards men. Some examples of how they manifest in relationships would be:

➤ Omission attitudes (not to take care of tasks that then women have to assume),

➤ To abuse the feminine capacity of looking after others,

➤ Make women responsible for the vitality of relationships,

➤ Control the relationship with distancing strategies,

➤ Lack of availability and lack of recognition that leave women with a hunger for affection.

Men, in their socialization, learn unconsciously to exert power upon women (they do not listen, their own desires come first, they treat the female body like an object). But times are changing and little by little more men are sensitive to those issues.

Effects of gender on women

Women are the ones who most suffer from the impact of the patriarchal system.

Feminine subjectivity is based on several ideals:

➤ To exist for the others: This means taking care of domestic tasks and taking care of others. Women adopt roles of housewife, mother, wife and ideal ways of being: receptive, nurturing contained, and available.

➤ Romantic love: Here the relationship becomes the first and main objective and even today it is deeply ingrained in women's psyches. The ideal for a woman is to belong to a man and often, to give priority to his projects before hers. Women grow up with the idea that love is central in their lives. When love goes away and they have not developed other resources, they get depressed. Love is more important than sex and we must not discount the role of religion that condemns the search for pleasure, specifically for women.

➤ High level of expectations placed on bonds and in taking care of others: This makes it difficult for women to find meaning through other experiences and places them in a vulnerable position and with excessive dependence on outer recognition. This dedication to look after relationships prevents her from dedicating herself to her professional objectives. It also means a lack of economic resources, which is linked to an economical and affective dependency. She often gets stuck in relationships that make her feel she is needed but that frustrate her, as they are not reciprocal.

➤ Idealization of a beauty stereotype: Women are led to believe that body beauty and youth are the necessary ingredients to be feminine, get the love of a man and be very happy. Body image then gets highly valued over intrapsychic aspects. Models and actresses are presented as a type of women who have everything: success, beauty, money and love. For most women, the impossibility of reaching this ideal provokes symptoms of inadequacy, anguish and uneasiness. As writer **Fatima Mernisi** says, the ideal of slimness and youth has become the burka for western women. To most women, slimness is associated with perfection and happiness. The difficulty for women to reach these ideals gets translated into body and emotional disorders. Often, doctors address these problems with pills and women are the ones who take more medicines (anti-depressants, tranquillizers, analgesics) than men. Instead of understanding it as one of the consequences of the system, it is read as a sign of weakness and inferiority and women feel very guilty. As we can see, the effects of gender on women's bodies are devastating. Both women and men suffer the effects of those ideals and the impossibility to attain them produces different symptoms in men and women's bodies.

New social trends

We are immersed in a period of change and transition.. At the same time that we live with the old stereotypes, these stereotypes are evolving. We do not talk about the family anymore but about families, which take their space in the social weaving. This proves that a new paradigm with new values is needed. The emphasis is not in the fact that a family is hetero or homosexual but in the quality of their bonding and the latest research points in this direction.

Masculine and feminine fade as rigid categories, which define opposite universes.

Father as the main authority figure and as the main provider is declining. Women going to work modify family relationships and allow some men to be more present in domestic tasks and emotionally available for their children.

Evidently, as in every process of change, transitions are not easy. Women have double working hours, some men resist losing their privileges and children relate to all kinds of gadgets and machines instead of people.

We have left behind the indissolubility of attachments for unstable relationships, or "liquid love" says **Irene Loyácomo**, an Argentinian psychoanalyst. Liquid love refers to relationships based on immediate satisfaction. Affective relationships cease to be forever, they become something you use, then throw away and substitute another one.

My experience as a therapist

In these twenty-three years of practice I have noticed some points I'd like to comment on regarding differences between men and women and how gender affects them.

My work with women patients

Requests for therapy have come mainly from women. It should not surprise us if we consider that women are the ones who most suffer the effects of the system. They are the ones who show more discomfort, the ones who evidence the suffering more in their bodies. There are some patterns that I see as a result of the gender system which have been constant and repetitive in many cases:

➤ A lack of self-esteem, of trust in their capacities.
➤ Ambivalence between the fear to be seen, to have a place in the world and the wish to be creative, to hold their projects and make them known.

➤ The inner tear between their wish to have a family and not to give up their working projects.

➤ The difficulty in recognising their own desires, as they were brought up to attend to the desires of others first.

➤ The difficulty finding a place of their own in the world so that having a place does not have to be exclusively through a relationship with a man.

➤ Feelings of body inadequacy. The need to work in the direction of having contact with the body more based on health, vitality, aliveness and spontaneity rather than on the beauty stereotype.

➤ Difficulty connecting with their own sexuality and the pleasure to enjoy it.

➤ Difficulty feeling a movement of their own, Lack of permission to move freely and explore the world.

My main interest has been to support women so that they could make contact with their bodies, their desires, their voice, their movement, their capacity to set up boundaries and to say no to relationships or situations that damage them. I give support so that they can take their own risks, to discern about their sexual desires and sexual choice and to help them open their body and emotional blockages, which had been structured in their childhood experiences.

I support the fact that a woman can live herself as subject of her own life and does not have to live it through others (partner, children).

I work to find in which ways her gender beliefs have limited her so she can open new paths.

Bioenergetic Analysis has been a powerful and precious tool to support all these processes, both in group sessions and in individual sessions. I have found that women, at some stage, often benefit by being in a therapy group with other women where they can find different models and ways to be a woman different from their mothers.

My work with male patients

I've tried to be attentive to how each one has been affected and limited by the prevailing model of masculinity and I have also found certain patterns:

➤ The difficulty to be in contact with their feelings. They are socialized to be much more in their heads than women, though we cannot generalize, only talk about repetitive patterns. Men fear to feel needy, weak, and impotent. They fear to lose control of their head.

➤ Fear of intimacy, disguised as being autonomous, fleeing attitude in relationships.

➤ Disconnectedness between feelings and sexuality.

➤ Difficulty to not only care for his own needs but to take the other's needs into account.

➤ Difficulty to connect with his own body, further than the stereotype of a strong powerful body. The body is often lived as a machine, a tool used to have a professional or a sexual achievement.

➤ Work is the main concern, sometimes, addiction to it.

➤ Difficulty to sustain uncertainty, to sustain the idea of process more than the final result.

➤ Difficulty to give up their privileged position and to open a more shared space, where they can listen, negotiate, leave space for the other. I must say that, little by little, men become aware of the high price they have to pay for this limiting stereotype of masculinity.

Our responsibility as bioenergetic analysts

What can we do as bioenergetic analysts to be open to the new types of family and to different sexual choices? How can we become sensitive to gender dynamics? I think we should move towards interrelatedness, the relational body dynamics that become present in our encounter with our clients and see the profound healing effects it can have. I have had good teachers who have taught me a way to make body energy dynamics and interrelatedness work together. I will mention some of them, such as Jean Marc Guillerme and the work of Virginia and Bob Hilton and Bob Lewis, who have found a way to enrich bioenergetics with these new approaches. They have taught me how important it is to be really present for the client and not only be aware of body dynamics.

I think it is crucial that we, as bioenergetic analysts, are sensitive and have the information and the necessary training on the issue of gender, sexual choices and new types of families, so that we can support our male and female patients when they explore the impact of those issues in their story and subjectivity.

We should reflect upon our beliefs concerning gender inequalities, about the roles and tasks distribution and about who cares for relationships. We need to revise our beliefs concerning power attitudes, domination and submission and how we can identify these patterns in affective relationships, first in our lives, then in our patients' lives. We need to be sensitive to the different ways gender affects women and men.

Bioenergetic Analysis needs to drink in these new approaches. We need to find a way to incorporate this knowledge to our valuable knowledge about energy, body and relational dynamics that we own as bioenergetic analysts. We need to emphasize more the impact of interrelatedness between therapist and client and the profound healing effects it can have. We should add these concepts to our practice, supervision and most important, to our training programs so that in our work we can feel open towards our clients, no matter what their sexual, affective choices are.

References

Benjamin, J. (1998) Pantheon books.
Bermejo, P. (2002) Reseña de M. Diamond: The shaping of masculinity, Aperturas Psicoanaliticas n° 19
Bonino, L. (1995) La violencia masculina en la pareja Paidós
Bonino, L. (1998) Los varones frente al cambio de las mujeres. Lectora, Revista de dones i intertextualitat
Bonino, L. (1987) Desvelando los micromachismos en la vida conyugal, Gel

Bonino, L. (2002) El caso de la violencia masculina Revista La Cibeles n° 2

Burin, M. (1987) Estudios sobre la subjetividad femenina Gel, Buenos Aires

Burin, M. (1996) Género y psicoanálisis: Subjetividades femeninas vulnerables Foro de Psicoanálisis y género.

Butler, J. (2002) Cuerpos que importan, Paidós

Carranza, M.E. (2004) Antropología y género: Breve revisión de algunas ideas Antropológicas sobre la mujer. www.psicomundo.com

Carril, E. (2000) Femenino/masculino, La pérdida de ideales y el duelo en Los duelos y sus destinos APU Montevideo. www.psicomundo.com

Carril, E. (2002) Un cuerpo en espera.el cuerpo en Psicoanálisis APU Montevideo.

Chodorow, N. (1978) The Reproduction of Mothering, University of California Press

Chodorow, N. (1994) Femininities, masculinities, sexualities Lexington univ. Press

Chodorow, N. (2003) El poder de los sentimientos, Paidós

Dio Bleichmar, E. (1998) Sexualidad femenina Paidós

Dio Bleichmar, E. (2002) Sexualidad y Género: Nuevas perspectivas en el psicoanálisis Contemporáneo en Aperturas,Revista de Psicoanálisis n° 11

Dimen, M. (2003) Sexuality, Intimacy, Power The Analitic Press, Hillsdale, NJ.

Errázuriz, P. (2008) Psicoanálisis y estudios de género Revista Humanidades y ciencias sociales. Santiago de Chile.

Fisher R. (1994) El caballero de la armadura oxidada, Obelisco,

Gil, E.P.(2002) Porqué le llaman género cuando quieren decir sexo: una aproximación a la teoria de la performatividad de Judith Butler,Atenea Digital n° 2 UAB,Barcelona

Kaufmann, M. (1994) Men, Feminism and Men's contradictory experiences of power. Sage Publications.

Lamas, M. (2007) Género: claridad y complejidad, en Adonde va la antropología, Mexico. www.psicomundo.com

Levinton, N. (2002) El superyo femenino Revista Aperturas Psicoanaliticas n° 1

Lopez, A. Guido, C. (2002) Aportes de los estudios de género en la conceptualizacion de la Masculinidad. Cátedra Libre en salud reproductiva, sexualidad y Genero.

Loyácomo, I. (2006) Inestabilidad del vínculo conyugal. Congreso dePsicoterapia sistemica, Buenos Aires www.redsistemica.com

Main, M. (2000) The organized categories of infant, child and adult attachment Journal of the American Psychoanalytical Association. Vol. 48,

Meler, I. (1996) La perspectiva de los estudios de género Subjetividad y cultura, México

Meler, I. (1997) Estados depresivos en pacientes mujeres, ídem www.psicomundo.com

Michalik, R. (2001) Interview with Judith Butler, revista Lola n° 2 www.lolapress.org

Money, J., Erhardt, A (1982) Desarrollo de la sexualidad humana.Madrid,Morata.

Quirici, T. (2000) El género hace al síntoma? APU Montevideo www.psicomundo.com

Stoller, R. (1968) Sex and Gender. Vol. 1,N.Y. Jason Aronson.

Truzzoli, C. (2007) Los prejuicios de género en las relaciones entre los sexos Revista Mujeres y salud n° 10

About the Author

Fina Pla is a licensed psychologist, a cbt and a supervisor. She is a member of ACAB (Associació Catalana en l'Anàlisi Bioenergètica). She has also been trained in Gestalt and in Psychoanalysis. She leads ALENAR Centre de Psicoteràpia in Barcelona, Spain.

Fina Pla
Alenar Centre de Psicoteràpia
Gran de Gracia 109-11,1er, 1ª
08012 Barcelona SPAIN
93-2172941 699754642
petxina@copc.es

Bioenergetic Analysis – The Clinical Journal of the International Institute for Bioenergetic Analysis (IIBA)

EDITORIAL OFFICE:
Dr. Vincentia Schroeter
PO Box 235738
Encinitas, Ca.
92023
email: vincentiaschroeter@gmail.com
email: vsschroeter@sbcglobal.net

EDITORIAL BOARD:
Vincentia Schroeter, PhD, Encinitas, Ca., USA
Margit Koemeda-Lutz, Dr., Zurich, Switzerland

Information and Instructions to Authors

1. The journal, BIOENERGETIC ANALYSIS, publishes clinical reports, theoretical analyses, empirical investigations, and book reviews pertaining to the theory and practice of Bioenergetic Analysis. Articles will be published in English. Two reviewers will evaluate the article on the basis of a blind review (all information pertaining to the author's identity will be omitted). The Editorial Board will also have a vote regarding the appropriateness of the article for inclusion in the journal.

2. Manuscripts should not have been published previously or been submitted elsewhere concomitantly. For manuscripts accepted for publication the copyright is automatically transferred to the publishing company, "Psychosozial-Verlag".

Manuscript Submission Guidelines

3. For submission please email text, figures and tables to the Chief Editor. For the next volume the editor is Vincentia Schroeter, PhD. Her email is: vincentiaschroeter@gmail.com. Her address is: Vincentia Schroeter, PhD, P. O. Box 235738, Encinitas, California, 92023, U. S. A.

4. FORMAL SET-UP OF MANUSCRIPTS:

A. 1ˢᵗ page:
1. Name(s) of author(s), title of paper, address for correspondence.
2. Summary (should not exceed half a typed page, double-spaced.
3. Key words (maximum 5)

B. 2ⁿᵈ and following pages:
1. Title of the paper (without name(s) of authors)
2. Text
3. References
4. Footnotes
5. Tables
6. Place each table and figure with captions on a separate page, and indicate where in your text they should be inserted.
7. Include information about the author(s) on a separate page.

C. Citations and References: When citing references, include the name(s) of the author(s) and the year of the publication in brackets. With more than 2 authors, the first author's name and "et al" will suffice. Examples are: Sachsse (1998) or Bacal & Newman (1994) or Streeck-Fischer et al. (2001).

D. References: All books and articles cited in the text, and only these, must be listed under "references" in alphabetical order in the following form:
1. Articles from journals: last name and first initial of first name of all authors, year of publication in brackets, title of the publication, name of the journal, volume number, which pages.
2. Articles from books: last name and first initial of first name of all authors or editors, year of publication in brackets, book title, publishing company, place of publication, which pages.
3. Example: Regli, D., Beiber, K., Mathier, F., & Grawe, K.

(2000): Beziehungsgestalttung und Aktivierung von Ressourcen in der Anfangsphase von Therapien. Verhaltensther Verhaltensmed 21, 399-420.

BIOENERGETIC ANALYSIS will be published once a year. Articles should be submitted before the fifteenth of September of the preceding year. Authors will be sent a notification of receipt of their manuscript within two weeks and will be informed about the status of their manuscripts, as to qualified acceptance or rejection, within two months after submission.

Original by M. Koemeda, modified 9/2007 by V. Schroeter

Psychosozial-Verlag

Hans-Jürgen Wirth

9/11 as a Collective Trauma

and other Essays
on Psychoanalysis and Society

Hans-Jürgen Wirth

Narcissism and Power

Psychoanalysis of Mental Disorders
in Politics

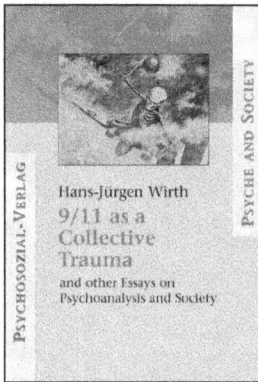

2004 · 198 pages · hardback
ISBN 978-3-89806-372-2

2009 · 266 pages · hardback
ISBN 978-3-89806-480-4

In 9/11 as a Collective Trauma Hans-Jürgen Wirth presents a collection of his most interesting essays about psyche and politics. He reflects on the psychic structure of suicide bombers and analyzes the psycho-political causes and the consequences of the Iraq War. The other essays focus on xenophobia and violence, the story of Jewish psychoanalysts who emigrated to the United States from Nazi Germany, and the idea of man in psychoanalysis.

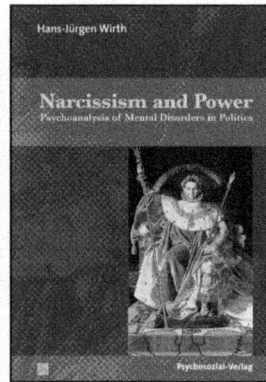

Social power is irresistibly appealing to narcissistically disturbed personalities. Uninhibited egocentricity, career obsession, a winning mentality and fantasies of grandeur – the narcissist employs these traits to clear the way through the corridors of economic and political power.

Blinded by his fantasies of grandeur and omnipotence, the narcissist loses his grasp on social reality and necessarily fails in the end. It is closely related to this loss of reality that the leader turns away from the norms, values and ideals to which he should actually be committed. Obsession with power, unscrupulousness and cynicism can give rise to brutal misanthropy.

Walltorstr. 10 · 35390 Giessen · Phone +49 641-969978-18 · Fax +49 641-969978-19
bestellung@psychosozial-verlag.de · www.psychosozial-verlag.de

Ralf Vogt

»Beseelbare« Therapy Objects

Psychoanalytic interactional approach
in a body- and trauma-oriented
psychotherapy

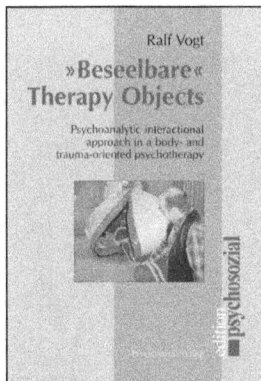

Ralf Vogt

Psychotrauma, State, Setting

Psychoanalytical-Action-Related Model
for a Treatment of Complexly Traumatized Patients (SPIM-20-CTP)

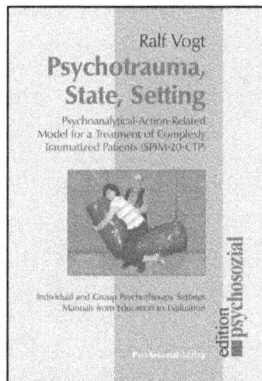

2006 · 187 pages · paperback
ISBN 978-3-89806-700-3

2008 · 337 pages · paperback
ISBN 978-3-89806-871-0

Ralf Vogt presents a new form of body therapy which may be applied as individual and as
group psychotherapy. The core of his original
concept are »beseelbare‹ objects«. With the
help of such objects, typical conflict situations
may be performed and problem-specific solutions may be playfully tested. The objects used
to that end – for example a cuddly cave into
which the patient may crawl – were specifically
designed for psychotherapeutic work by the author. These »beseelbare‹ therapy objects« are
an important aid to get access to any blocked
or buried affects of the patients.

Ralf Vogt presents a complete conception of
a psychotraumatological treatment which is
applicable to complex traumatized patients
(representing the majority of psychotrauma
disorders in ambulant practices) as well as to
other patients. His very structured procedure
with theoretical derivations, including many
handouts for clients and treaters, and specific
case vignettes, is unique and important in its
compactness to the point of evaluation. The
book is suitable reading for therapists and advisors, and also for advanced patients.

Walltorstr. 10 · 35390 Giessen · Phone +49 641-969978-18 · Fax +49 641-969978-19
bestellung@psychosozial-verlag.de · www.psychosozial-verlag.de

Psychosozial-Verlag

H. Shmuel Erlich,
Mira Erlich-Ginor, Hermann Beland

Fed with Tears – Poisoned with Milk

The »Nazareth« Group-Relations-Conferences. Germans and Israelis – The Past in the Present

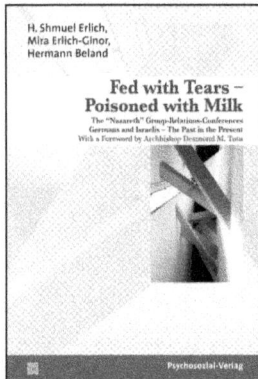

Lynne Lehrman Weiner (Ed.)

Sigmund Freud Through Lehrman's Lens

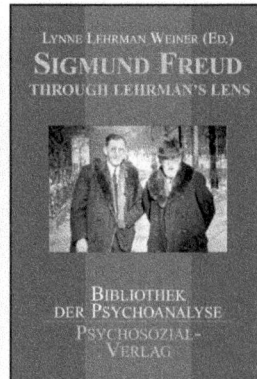

2009 · 192 pages · paperback
ISBN 978-3-89806-751-5

2008 · 222 pages · paperback
ISBN 978-3-89806-841-3

This volume aims to make a unique and significant contribution to the proliferating literature on German-Israeli relatedness in the post-Holocaust era. It is both a record and a testimony to a novel and vitally important approach to this work, demonstrating the possibility of dealing with Germans and Israelis in a way that is immediate, direct, and powerfully evocative. Its power lies in that it is not work aimed at rapprochement or exoneration. It focuses on the two groups by using highly skilled and trained professionals – psychoanalysts and psychotherapists – from both countries.

This book is based on 16-millimeter amateur films by the psychoanalyst Philip Lehrman who shot these in the 1920s, during his analysis with Freud. A documentary was produced from the films with an accompanying commentary by Lehrman. Almost 50 years after his death, his daughter Lynne Lehrman Weiner published the transcription of the documentary film and a large number of selected stills in the form of an illustrated book. The result allows a very personal view of the prominent figures of classical psychoanalysis and an insight into »their« Europe of the 1920s. It is winner of Gradiva Award, 2009!

Walltorstr. 10 · 35390 Giessen · Phone +49 641-969978-18 · Fax +49 641-969978-19
bestellung@psychosozial-verlag.de · www.psychosozial-verlag.de